Francis Asbury's America

Francis Asbury Publishing Company was founded in 1980 by several members of the Asbury community in Wilmore, Kentucky. Its aim was to meet the spiritual needs of that segment of the evangelical Christian public that is Wesleyan in outlook and to communicate the Wesleyan message to the larger Christian community.

In 1983 Francis Asbury Publishing Company became a part of Zondervan Publishing House. Its aim remains the spread of the Wesleyan message through the publication of popular, practical, and scholarly books for all Wesleyan denominations.

FRANCIS ASBURY PRESS
Box 7
Wilmore, Kentucky 40390

Francis Asbury's America

An Album of Early American Methodism

Compiled and Edited by Terry D. Bilhartz

FRANCIS ASBURY PRESS
of Zondervan Publishing House
1415 Lake Dr. S.E. • Grand Rapids, MI 49506

FRANCIS ASBURY'S AMERICA
Copyright © 1984 by The Zondervan Corporation,
Grand Rapids, Michigan

FRANCIS ASBURY PRESS is an imprint of Zondervan Publishing House,
1415 Lake Drive, SE, Grand Rapids, Michigan 49506

Library of Congress Cataloging in Publication Data

Asbury, Francis, 1745-1816.
   Francis Asbury's America.

   Includes index.
     1. Asbury, Francis, 1745-1816.   2. Methodist Church—
United States—Bishops—Biography.   3.   United States—
Description and travel—To 1783.   4.   United States—
Description and travel—1783-1848.   5.   Methodist Church—
United States—History—18th century.   6. Methodist
Church—United States—History—19th century.
I. Bilhartz, Terry D.   II. Title.
BX8495.A8A33   1984   287'.632'0924 [B]   83-25945
ISBN 0-310-44790-9
ISBN 0-310-44791-7 (pbk.)

Cover reproduction: Frederic Edwin Church, "Hooker and Company Journeying Through the Wilderness from Plymouth to Hartford, in 1636," (1846)
source unknown, pre 1850. Used by permission of Wadsworth Atheneum.

Printed in the United States of America

84 85 86 87 88 89 90 / 10 9 8 7 6 5 4 3 2 1

IN APPRECIATION

I owe much to the many people who contributed their time and talents
in the preparation of this book. First I thank the officials at following
institutions for making their resources so readily available: American
Philosophical Society; Drew University Library; John Street Museum, New
York; Library of Congress; Lovely Lane Museum, Baltimore; Maryland
Historical Society; New York Public Library; Presbyterian Historical Society,
Philadelphia; St. George's Museum, Philadelphia; Sam Houston State
University Library; Texas A&M University Library; and the University of
Pennsylvania Library. I also extend my personal thanks to Lyman Coleman
for suggesting the project; Richard Beeman and the Philadelphia Center
for Early American Studies for a travel grant to offset the costs of research;
Tom and Shirley Hershberger of tom/design graphics for their hours of labor
with the layout, design, and copy preparation; Georgette Grey of CrazyQuilt
Graphics for the typesetting; and Patty Ann Bilhartz for her support and
assistance in every stage of preparation. Finally, it is with affection that
I dedicate this book to Paul and Ann Morell, authentic Methodists who
have dared to follow in the Asburian tradition.

CONTENTS

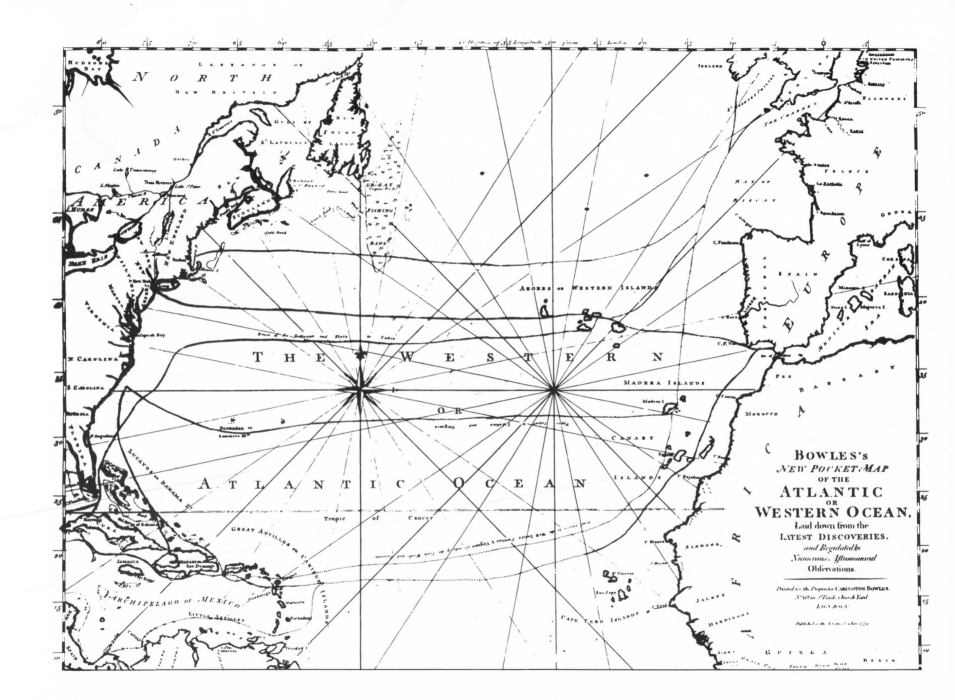

BOWLES's
NEW POCKET-MAP
OF THE
ATLANTIC
OR
WESTERN OCEAN,
Laid down from the
LATEST DISCOVERIES,
and Regulated by
*Numerous Astronomical
Observations.*

Printed for the Proprietor CARINGTON BOWLES,
No 69 in St Pauls Church Yard,
LONDON

Published as the Act directs, 1790

FOREWORD

The history of early American Methodism is largely the history of Francis Asbury. As the charismatic father and bishop of the Methodist Episcopal Church, Asbury held greater ecclesiastical powers than any Protestant in early national America. Alone, without check from any lay or clerical body, he defined the circuits and assigned the Methodist itinerants their charges. Counting the life and health of the ordained as the property of God, he placed rigorous demands upon his men. Some balked, but generally his personal self-sacrifice diffused complaint. During his forty-five year American ministry between 1771 and 1816, Asbury travelled on horseback 270,000 miles, preached 16,500 sermons, presided over 240 annual conferences, and ordained 4,000 preachers. And under his supervision, Methodism grew from the smallest to the largest American denomination.

Three weeks after Asbury's death, Reverend Ezekiel Cooper addressed a crowd of three to four thousand mourners who jammed into Philadelphia's Old St. George's Church. Standing behind the black-shrouded pulpit, in the same house where forty-five years earlier Asbury preached his first American sermon, Cooper announced that the "venerable father" was dead, and that his passing was "one of the most distressing and trying occurrences . . . ever befallen the Methodist Episcopal Church . . . the like never will, perhaps, never can befall us again." Asbury had attained his heavenly reward, Cooper asserted, and now the church must emulate his saintly example. The tearful audience was keenly aware that Asbury's death marked the end of an era.

This volume, based upon the journal of the "father of American Methodism," celebrates the Age of Asbury. It was an era of revolution and restoration, of conservatism and reform, of sectarian rivalry and ecumenical harmony, of expansion and consolidation. But most of all, for Methodism it was an era of evangelical fervor and missionary enterprise, the zeal of which never has been surpassed.

BIRTH and BOYHOOD

Asbury hailed from the Black Country of Staffordshire, England. This coal mining and iron forging region three thousand miles from the American shore was notorious, but not for producing saints. The Black Country was a land of colliers, ironworkers, chain makers, and turn nailers. It was a region populated by laborers who spent their working days in the dirt and grime of the mines and forges and their nights and holidays in the local pubs where they drank cheap ale, told tall tales, and gambled on cockfights.

Never a stereotypical Black Countryman, young Francis was almost a newcomer to the region. His paternal grandfather and namesake, Francis Aspbury [sic], grew up near Litchfield, about twenty-five miles outside the industrial district of the Black Country. In 1706, the elder Francis married Sarah Mulliner and settled in the village of Alrewas. Here they reared a family of five boys, including Joseph, the future father of the American bishop.

The elder Francis owned a small plot, but it was too tiny to provide an adequate inheritance for all his surviving sons. Consequently the Aspbury family scattered. Joseph, the youngest and perhaps least endowed, moved the greatest distance. He settled between West Bromwich and Wednesbury, about four miles to the north of Birmingham, finding employment as a gardener for two of the wealthy ironmasters in the parish. At age twenty-one, Joseph married Elizabeth Rogers of Walsall. In April 1743, Elizabeth gave birth to their first daughter, whom they named Sarah in honor of Joseph's mother. Twenty-eight months later, their second and last child, Francis Asbury, was born.

"RECOLLECTIONS" TAKEN FROM ASBURY'S JOURNAL ENTRIES OF JULY 16, 1792, JULY 24, 1774, AND SEPTEMBER 12, 1771.

I was born in Old England, near the foot of Hampstead Bridge, in the parish of Handsworth, about four miles from Birmingham, in Staffordshire, and according to the best of my after-knowledge on the 20th or 21st day of August, in the year of our Lord 1745.

My father's name was Joseph, and my mother's, Elizabeth Asbury: they were people in common life; were remarkable for honesty and industry, and had all things needful to enjoy; had my father been as saving as laborious, he might have been wealthy. As it was, it was his province to be employed as a farmer and gardener by the two richest families in the parish.

I was sent to school early, and began to read the Bible between six and seven years of age, and greatly delighted in the

ASBURY'S BIRTHPLACE
"NEAR THE FOOT OF HAMPSTEAD BRIDGE."

ungodly families we had in the parish: here I became vain, but not openly wicked.

Some months after this I returned home and made my choice, when about thirteen years and a half old to learn a branch of business at which I wrought about six and a half [years]: during this time I enjoyed great liberty, and in the family was once more treated more like a son or an equal than an apprentice.

BIRMINGHAM: HOME OF THE BOULTON AND WATT STEAM ENGINE

IRONMAN AT WORK

historical part of it. My schoolmaster was a great churl, and used to beat me cruelly; this drove me to prayer, and it appeared to me, that God was near to me. My father having but the one son, greatly desired to keep me at school, he cared not how long: but in this design he was disappointed; for my master, by his severity, had filled me with such horrible dread, that with me anything was preferable to going to school. I lived some time in one of the wealthiest and most

9

THE CALLING

When between thirteen and fourteen years of age, the Lord visited my soul again. I then found myself more inclined to obey and carefully attend preaching in West Bromwich; so that I heard Stillingfleet, Bagnel, Ryland, Anderson, Mansfield, and Talbott, men who preached the truth. I then began to watch over my inward and outward conduct; and having a desire to hear the Methodists, I went to Wednesbury, and heard Mr. Fletcher and Mr. Ingham, but did not understand them, though one of their subjects is fresh in my memory to this day.

MANWOOD COTTAGE, HANDSWORTH, ENGLAND,
SITE OF ASBURY'S FIRST SERMON

JOHN WESLEY

The next year Mr. Mather came into those parts. I was then about fifteen; and, young as I was, the Word of God soon made deep impressions on my heart, which brought me to Jesus Christ, who graciously justified my guilty soul through faith in his precious blood; and soon showed me the excellency and necessity of holiness. About sixteen I experienced a marvellous display of the grace of God, which some might think was full sanctification, and was indeed very happy, though in an ungodly family. At about seventeen I began to hold some public meetings; and between seventeen and eighteen began to exhort and preach. When about twenty-one I went through Staffordshire and Gloucestershire, in the place of a travelling preacher; and the next year through Bedfordshire, Sussex, &c. In 1769 I was appointed assistant in Northamptonshire; and the next year travelled in Wiltshire.

ELIZABETH ASBURY

From Bristol I went home to acquaint my parents with my great undertaking, which I opened in as gentle a manner as possible. Though it was grievous to flesh and blood, they consented to let me go. My mother is one of the tenderest parents in the world; but, I believe, she was blessed in the present instance with Divine assistance to part with me.

I returned to Bristol in the latter end of August, where Richard Wright was waiting for me, to sail in a few days for Philadelphia. When I came to Bristol I had not one penny of money; but the Lord soon opened the hearts of friends, who supplied me with clothes and ten pounds: thus I found, by experience, that the Lord will provide for those who trust in him.

On the 7th of August, 1771, the Conference began at Bristol, in England. Before this, I had felt for half a year strong intimations in my mind that I should visit America; which I laid before the Lord, being unwilling to do my own will, or to run before I was sent. During this time my trials were very great, which the Lord, I believe, permitted to prove and try me, in order to prepare me for future usefulness. At the Conference it was proposed that some preachers should go over to the American continent. I spoke my mind, and made an offer of myself. It was accepted by Mr. Wesley and others, who judged I had a call.

BRISTOL, FROM ST. AUGUSTINE'S QUAY

CROSSING THE ATLANTIC

1771 On *Wednesday, September 4*, we set sail from a port near Bristol and having a good wind, soon passed the channel. For three days I was very ill with the seasickness; and no sickness I ever knew was equal to it.

Thursday, 12. I will set down a few things that lie on my mind. Whither am I going? To the New World. What to do? To gain honour? No, if I know my own heart. To get money? No: I am going to live to God, and to bring others so to do. In America there has been a work of God: some moving first amongst the Friends, but in time it declined: likewise by the Presbyterians, but amongst them also it declined. The people God owns in England, are the Methodists. The doctrines they preach, and the discipline they enforce are, I believe, the purest of any people now in the world. The Lord has greatly blessed these doctrines and this discipline in the three kingdoms: they must therefore be pleasing to him.

"I feel my spirit bound to the New World, and my heart united to the people, though unknown: and have great cause to believe that I am not running before I am sent."
Francis Asbury
September 21, 1771

Lord's Day, September 29. I preached to the ship's company again, on these words, "To you is the word of this salvation sent." I felt some drawings of soul towards them, but saw no fruit. Yet still I must go on.

Tuesday, October 13. Though it was very windy, I fixed my back against the mizenmast and preached freely on those well-known words, 2 Cor. v, 20: "Now then we are ambassadors for Christ, as though God did beseech you by us: we pray you in Christ's stead, be ye reconciled to God." I felt the power of truth on my soul, but still, alas! saw no visible fruit. . . . Many have been my trials in the course of this voyage; from the want of a proper bed, and proper provisions, from seasickness, and from being surrounded with men and women ignorant of God, and very wicked. But all this is nothing. If I cannot bear this, what have I learned? O, I have reason to be much ashamed of many things, which I speak and do before God and man. Lord, pardon my manifold defects and failures in duty.

AN EIGHTEENTH CENTURY VESSEL ENROUTE TO AMERICA

HISTORICAL PERSPECTIVES

1703 — John Wesley is born in Epworth, England.

1735 — Revival under the preaching of Jonathan Edwards in Northampton, Massachusetts, inaugurates the era of the "Great Awakening."

1739 — John Wesley establishes "united societies" to nurture young Christians toward spiritual maturity.

1745 — Francis Asbury is born in Staffordshire, England.

1754 — George Washington with 200 militia attempts to drive the French from the Ohio River Valley. The confrontation sparks a global conflict known in America as the French and Indian War.

1763 — Treaty of Paris ends the French and Indian War. England acquires new land in America, but also is left with heavy post-war debts.

1765 — Colonists boycott British goods in protest against the revenue-raising Stamp Act.

1769 — Richard Boardman and Joseph Pilmoor arrive as Wesley's first missionaries to America.

1770 — The Boston Massacre. Eight Americans are slain as British Redcoats fire into a Boston street mob.

1771 — Francis Asbury sails for America.

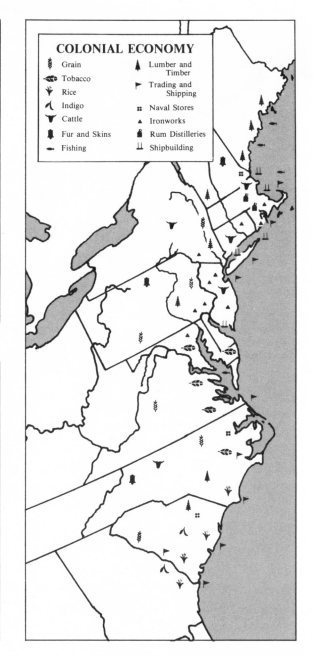

COLONIAL ECONOMY

- Grain
- Tobacco
- Rice
- Indigo
- Cattle
- Fur and Skins
- Fishing
- Lumber and Timber
- Trading and Shipping
- Naval Stores
- Ironworks
- Rum Distilleries
- Shipbuilding

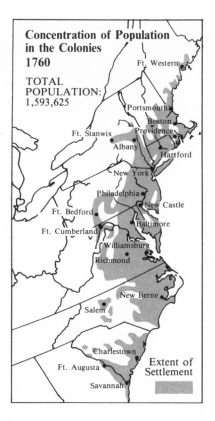

Concentration of Population in the Colonies 1760

TOTAL POPULATION: 1,593,625

Ft. Western
Portsmouth
Boston
Providence
Ft. Stanwix
Albany
Hartford
New York
Philadelphia
Ft. Bedford
New Castle
Baltimore
Ft. Cumberland
Williamsburg
Richmond
New Berne
Salem
Charlestown
Ft. Augusta
Savannah

Extent of Settlement

EARLY AMERICAN MINISTRY

At twenty-six years, the youngest of Wesley's foreign missionaries, Asbury embarked for America glowing with youthful enthusiasm. His early experiences on the continent reinforced his high expectations. Just three weeks after arrival, Asbury already had concluded that the Americans were "more willing to hear the Word than the English." Asbury maintained this conviction throughout his American ministry.

Of course Asbury's perfectionist eyes also spotted the spiritual shortcomings of the colonists. At a glance he noticed that the Americans were too attached to the things of the world to give as liberally as they ought. And he complained that too many were lax in their enforcement of Methodist rules, while too few yearned for the blessing of perfect love. Even more alarming, Asbury disapproved of the reluctance of his itinerant colleagues to leave the cities. No matter how great the risk or hopeless

the task, Asbury believed his mission was to spread the tidings of salvation across the fertile, yet virgin land.

Bold and stubborn, Asbury determined to show his colleagues the true Wesleyan way. With little regard for the weather, Asbury set out across hill and vale, travelling an extra ten or twenty miles daily, just to reach another house and preach another message. Wherever he went, Asbury established new classes and societies, even as he pruned existing rolls until they reflected only those willing to abide by the rigors of Methodist discipleship. His disciplinarian bent cost him initial popularity, and on several occasions his insistent travel almost cost him his life. Yet in time his reputation as a resolute travelling evangelist won him lasting respect. And his circuit-riding zeal gave credibility to that old adage, "No one's out today but crows and Methodist preachers."

1771 *Tuesday, October 27.* This day we landed in Philadelphia, where we were directed to the house of one Mr. Francis Harris, who kindly entertained us in the evening, and brought us to a large church, where we met with a considerable congregation. Brother Pilmoor preached. The people looked on us with pleasure, hardly know-*

ing how to show their love sufficiently, bidding us welcome with fervent affection, and receiving us as angels of God. O that we may always walk worthy of the vocation wherewith we are called!

1772 *Tuesday, April 28. I intended to go out of town; but could not get a horse. So I stayed for*

*For the sake of clarity, days and dates have been added and obscure passages have been lightly edited.

REV. JOSEPH PILMOOR

PHILADELPHIA

Brother Wright, and heard that many were offended at my shutting them out of society meeting, as they had been greatly indulged before. But this does not trouble me. While I stay, the rules must be attended to; and I cannot suffer myself to be guided by halfhearted Methodists.

Monday, October 19. Set off in the stage for Philadelphia. The company was all pretty quiet, except one young man, who frequently profaned the name of the Lord. It was my intention to reprove him; but waiting for a proper time, I found an opportunity when there was only one person with him, and then told him how he had grieved me. He received the admonition very well; and excused himself by saying he did not think of what he was doing. Afterward he seemed more careful.

ASBURY PREACHING AT ST. GEORGE'S CHURCH

ST. GEORGE'S CHURCH, PHILADELPHIA

1773 Wednesday, April 14. Came very weary to Philadelphia; but the sight of my friends greatly revived me; and all seem to be in peace.

Thursday, 15. I preached for the first time, on this visit in Philadelphia, on Ruth ii, 4. Many people attended, and the Lord filled my heart with holy gladness. All things are in peace here.

NEW YORK METHODISM

The first New York Methodists consisted of eight to ten German Palatine families who emigrated in 1760 from Limerick County, Ireland. Though their numbers included Philip Embury, a licensed local preacher, the early Methodists failed to establish a class or society for six years. In October 1766, however, Mrs. Barbara Heck, a long-standing Methodist deeply concerned with the decaying spiritual health of her friends, spotted a band of Palatine men playing openly with a deck of cards. Infuriated at this flagrantly indecent behavior, Heck stormed after Embury and admonished him for his lack of duty. "Philip, you must preach to us," she asserted, "or we shall go to hell, and God will require our blood at your hands." "How can I preach?" returned Embury. "I have neither house nor congregation." "Preach," Mrs. Heck replied, "in your own house, and to your own company."

Embury accepted Mrs. Heck's challenge, and preached his first American sermon in his home to a congregation of five. Soon increasing crowds demanded a relocation to a larger "upper room" on Barrack Street near the British military headquarters. By early 1767, the growing party moved again, this time to a narrow room on William Street which previously had served as a rigging loft. The infant congregation remained at the "Rigging Loft" until October 1768, when they purchased a tract of land on John Street and built Wesley Chapel. By the time Asbury arrived in the fall of 1771, some two hundred New Yorkers worshipped regularly at the chapel and the prospects for continued growth remained high.

BARBARA HECK BREAKS UP THE CARD GAME

RICHARD BOARDMAN

1771 *November 11. On Monday I set out for New York, and found Richard Boardman there in peace, but weak in body. Now I must apply myself to my old work—to watch, and fight, and pray. Lord, help!*

Tuesday, 12. I preached in New York to a large congregation on I Cor. ii, 2. . . . I approved much of the spirit of the people: they were loving and serious; there appeared also, in some, a love of discipline. Though I was unwilling to go to New York so soon, I believe it is all well, and I still hope I am in the order of God.

Tuesday, 19. I remain in New York, though unsatisfied with our being both in town together. I have not yet the thing which I seek—a circulation of preachers, to avoid partiality and popularity. However, I am fixed to the Methodist plan, and do what I do faithfully as to God.

Thursday, 21. At present I am dissatisfied. I judge we are to shut up in the cities this winter. My brethren seem unwilling to leave the cities, but I think I shall show them the way.

1772 _Tuesday, March 10. New York is a large city, and well situated for trade; but the streets and buildings are very irregular. The inhabitants are of various denominations, but nevertheless of a courteous and sociable disposition. There are several places of Divine Worship: the Episcopalians have three; the High Dutch, one; the Low Dutch, three; the Lutherans, two; the French Protestants, one; the Presbyterians, two; the Seceders, one; the Baptists, one; the Moravians, one; the Methodists, one; and the Jews, one. The city abounds with inhabitants; but the exact number I could not ascertain._

WESLEY CHAPEL—DESIGNED AND BUILT BY PHILIP EMBURY

RIGGING LOFT

Sunday, September 13. After preaching to many people on the Lord's Day at seven, I prepared to approach the table. There was a great drawing among the people while these words were enforced: "This do in remembrance of me." Lord, prepare my heart. My bleeding Lord! let my soul feel thy melting love. Lord, make all thy people glad together in thee, that thou mayest be glorified in and by us both now and ever.

At the table I was greatly affected with the sight of the poor Negroes, seeing their sable faces at the table of the Lord. In the evening I had a full house and much Divine assistance.

Saturday, October 10. I received a letter from Mr. Wesley, in which he required a strict attention to discipline; and appointed me to act as assistant.*

*The duties of an "assistant" were roughly equivalent to the duties of a modern day "district superintendent."

PETER WILLIAMS—EARLY METHODIST
PREACHER, NEW YORK

pertaining to the society. This afforded me great satisfaction, and more especially the revival of religion, which has lately taken place in the city.

1774 *Saturday, September 17.* In meeting the bands, I showed them the impropriety and danger of keeping their thoughts or fears of each other to themselves: this frustrates the design of bands; produces coolness and jealousies towards each other; and is undoubtedly the policy of Satan.

1773 *Lord's Day, June 13.* I preached this morning to a considerable number of people. Mr. Rankin found his spirits raised, and was much comforted. In the afternoon Mr. Rankin, Capt. Webb, Mr. Wright, and myself went to St. Paul's church, and received the sacrament.

Wednesday, 23. On my return to New York, I found Mr. Rankin had been well employed in settling matters

CAPTAIN THOMAS WEBB

THOMAS RANKIN

Lord's Day, November 6. Both my body and mind were afflicted today. In the morning I showed the congregation the danger of settling on their lees; as all do who rest in dead formality, or trust in any past experience. In the evening, I addressed the people on the heartfelt inquiry of the trembling jailor, "What must I do to be saved?"

WESLEY CHAPEL, JOHN STREET, NEW YORK CITY

1772 *Friday, February 21.* Having a desire to visit my friends on Staten Island, I set off in the afternoon of the 21st, contrary to the persuasion of my friends in New York. Samuel Selby who was tender towards me in my illness, and took care of me as if I had been his father, accompanied me.

Justice Wright received us and entertained us kindly; and though weak and weary, I preached at Peter Van Pelt's to a few persons, with much satisfaction. Mr. Disosway (a man of fortune) invited me to preach in his house, to which I consented; and Justice Wright sent us there on the Lord's Day, with several of his family. I preached twice at that gentleman's house to a large company. Some, it appeared, had not heard a sermon for half a year; such a famine there is of the Word in these parts, and a still greater one of the <u>pure</u> Word.

Monday, February 24. My labours increase, and my strength is renewed. Though I came here weak, yet after preaching three times I felt myself strong.

AN 18TH CENTURY EXECUTION

Thanks be to God, who hath raised me up from so low a state!

Thursday, April 30. Set out for Philadelphia; but about a mile from the city found that the bridge could not be crossed on horseback; so I left my horse and walked to the ferry. Brother Wright took the horse and went to Burlington on his way to New York. I desired to attend the execution of the prisoners at Chester, and John King went with me. We found them penitent: and two of the four obtained peace with God, and seemed very thankful. I preached with liberty to a great number of people under the jail wall. The sheriff was friendly and very kind. John King preached at the gallows to a vast multitude; after which I prayed with them. The executioner pretended to tie them all up, but only tied one, and let the rest fall. One of them was a young man about fifteen. We saw them all afterward, and exhorted them to be careful.

Monday, October 19. After dining at New Brunswick, we came to Princeton, a place I had long wished to see for the sake of the pious Mr. Davies, late president of the college there. Here I met Mr. Boardman, and we both agreed in judgment about the affairs of the society; and were comforted together.

ABERDEEN

BALTIMORE

ANNAPOLIS

Lord's Day, December 6. Went about five miles to preach in our first meetinghouse [Bush Forest Chapel]. The house had no windows or doors; the weather was very cold: so that my heart pitied the people when I saw them so exposed. Putting a handkerchief over my head, I preached, and after an hour's intermission (the people waiting all the time in the cold) I preached again.

1773 *Lord's Day, February 21. The weather was excessively severe, yet many people came to hear the Word at Joseph Presbury's. I rode about six or seven miles to preach in the Gunpowder Neck, but never felt colder weather. The water froze as it ran from the horse's nostrils; and a friend said the water froze as it came from his eyes. However, after preaching to a few people, I returned.*

BUSH FOREST CHAPEL, 1769,
NEAR ABERDEEN, MD.
SECOND CHAPEL IN MARYLAND
BUILT BY ROBERT STRAWBRIDGE

Lord's Day, September 5. In the morning I preached at [Baltimore] town, and then at the Point, where the people seem more attentive; and afterward returned to town, and preached at night to a large congregation. It is a matter of great grief to me, to see the inhabitants of this town so much devoted to pride, spiritual idolatry, and almost

JOHN KING PREACHING THE FIRST METHODIST
SERMON IN BALTIMORE

every species of sin. Lord, visit them yet in tender mercy, to reform and save their souls.

Thursday, November 25. Had occasion to go to Annapolis, and found some desire to preach there. But perceiving the spirit and practice of the people, I declined it. A tavern keeper offered me the use of his house for preaching; but he was a Deist, and I did not feel free to open my mouth in his house.

THE GERMAN CHURCH, BALTIMORE—MOTHER CHURCH
FOR THE UNITED BRETHREN

1774 *Lord's Day, March 27.* My indisposition and weakness of body have so pressed me down for some time past, that I do not expect to abide long in this world of danger and trouble; neither do I desire it. But, come life or come death, let the will of the Lord be done!

Lord's Day, April 3. Though still very unwell, I attempted to preach. How difficult it is for a man who longs for the salvation of souls to be silent!

Tuesday, May 3. Had a friendly intercourse with Mr. Otterbein and Mr. Swope, the German ministers, respecting the plan of Church discipline on which they intended to proceed. They agreed to imitate our methods as nearly as possible.

Thursday, May 19. I am happy in God after all my labours. But when amongst my friends, my mind inclines to a degree of cheerfulness bordering on levity. O for more watchfulness!—a more constant, striking sense of an omnipresent God!

PHILIP WILLIAM OTTERBEIN,
FOUNDER OF THE
UNITED BRETHREN

Tuesday, June 14. My heart seems wholly devoted to God, and he favours me with power over all outward and inward sin. . . . Some people, if they felt as I feel at present, would perhaps conclude they were saved from all indwelling sin. O my God, save me and keep me every moment of my life!

> "I still pray, and long, and wait, for an outpouring of the blessed spirit on this town. O that the time were come! Lord, hasten it for thy mercy's sake!"
>
> Francis Asbury,
> Baltimore, December 28, 1773

TROUBLED TIMES, 1775-1783

After years of worsening relations, on April 19, 1775, British Redcoats engaged a band of American Minutemen near the Lexington bridge. For fifteen months an undeclared war raged. Then on the 2nd (not the 4th) of July, 1776, the Second Continental Congress severed final ties with the motherland by declaring the colonies to be "free and independent states."

The American Revolution was a civil war which pitted colonist against colonist. Loyalists swearing allegiance to the King suffered intense persecution at the hands of the Patriots espousing the cause of liberty. Among those suspected of Tory sympathies were Anglican churchmen, a group which in 1775 included 3,148 members of Methodist societies.

John Wesley aggravated an already delicate situation when he published an indiscreet attack against the patriot cause. This political pamphlet, ironically entitled *A Calm Address*, intensified the anti-Methodist protest. Often insulted, threatened, and imprisoned, one by one Methodist missionaries returned to England. Among Wesley's appointees, only Asbury remained, and even he was forced to spend a great portion of the war years in hiding.

The war disrupted Methodist circuits and turned meetinghouses into makeshift hospitals. In some colonies it silenced Methodist preaching and drove societies underground. But troubled times could not quench the fires of revival. By the war's end, Methodist membership had soared upwards toward 15,000—an increase of over 450% in only eight years.

GEORGE III,
KING OF ENGLAND,
1760-1820

THE BATTLE OF LEXINGTON, APRIL 19, 1775

1775 *Lord's Day, April 30. We have alarming military accounts from Boston, New York, and Philadelphia. Surely the Lord will overrule, and make all these things subservient to the spiritual welfare of his Church.*

Monday, August 7. I received a letter from Mr. Thomas Rankin, in which he informed me that himself, Mr. Rodda, and Mr. Dempster had consulted, and deliberately concluded it would be best to return to England. But I can by no means agree to leave such a field for gathering souls to Christ, as we have in America. It would be an eternal dishonour to the Methodists, that we should all leave three thousand souls, who desire to commit themselves to our care; neither is it the part of

23

STATEHOUSE, PHILADELPHIA (INDEPENDENCE HALL)

Tuesday, April 16. A friend from New York informed us, that troops were raised and entrenchments made in that city. O Lord, we are oppressed; undertake for us.

Wednesday, July 31. . . . The English ships have been coasting to and fro, watching for some advantages: but what can they expect to accomplish without an army of two or three hundred thousand men? And even then, there would be but little prospect of their success.

a good shepherd to leave his flock in time of danger: therefore, I am determined, by the grace of God, not to leave them. Let the consequence be what it may.

1776 *Tuesday, March 19.* I also received an affectionate letter from Mr. Wesley, and am truly sorry that man ever dipped into the politics of America. . . . Had he been a subject of America, no doubt but he would have been as zealous an advocate of the American cause. But some inconsiderate persons have taken occasion to censure the Methodists in America, on acccount of Mr. Wesley's political sentiments.

THE RUINS OF TRINITY CHURCH, NEW YORK.
FIRE SET BY AMERICAN PATRIOTS IN PROTEST OF BRITISH EXECUTION OF NATHAN HALE, SEPTEMBER, 1776

PULLING DOWN A STATUE OF GEORGE III

BRITISH REDCOATS MARCH INTO NEW YORK CITY, 1776

O that this dispensation might answer its proper end! that the people would fear the Lord, and sincerely devote themselves to his service! Then, no doubt, wars and bloodshed would cease.

Lord's Day, September 1. Many immortal souls are driven to eternity by the bloody sword. This is a grief to my soul! Lord, scatter them that delight in war and thirst for human blood!

1777 *Wednesday, April 16. Riding after preaching to R.P.'s, my chaise was shot through; but the Lord preserved my person. The war is now at such a height, that they are pressing men for the sea service.*

Monday, October 13. These distressing times have lately induced many people to pay a more diligent attention to the things of God. So I have hopes that these temporal troubles will prepare the way for spiritual blessings.

1778 *Friday, March 13. I was under some heaviness of mind. But it was no wonder: three thousand miles from home—my friends have left me—I am considered by some as an enemy of the country—every day liable to be seized by violence, and abused. However, all this is but a trifle to suffer for Christ, and the salvation of souls. Lord, stand by me!*

Saturday, April 11. From March 10, 1778, on conscientious principles I was a non-juror, and could not preach in the State of Maryland; and therefore withdrew to the Delaware State, where the clergy were not required to take the State oath: though, with a clear conscience I could have taken the oath of the Delaware State, had it been required; and would have done it, had I not been prevented by a tender fear of hurting the scrupulous consciences of others.

BARRATT'S CHAPEL, NEAR FREDERICA, DELAWARE

THE PERSECUTION OF
TORY LOYALISTS

1779 *March 19. On Friday I was inclined to believe, that the night before the Lord had resanctified my soul. . . . I fear I have been too slack in urging both myself and others to diligently seek the experience of this great and blessed gift. May the Lord help me from this time, to live free from outward and inward sin, always maintaining the spirit of the Gospel in meekness, purity, and love!*

1780 *Saturday, January 1. Now commences the new year; these two years past have been trying years to me, and I doubt not but this will be so likewise; only, my God keep me through the water and fire, and let me rather die than live to sin against thee!*

Monday, April 24. Rode to Baltimore, and my friends were much rejoiced to see me; but silence broke my heart. The act against non-jurors reduced me to silence, because the oath of

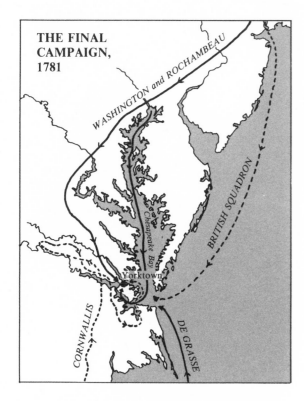

THE FINAL
CAMPAIGN,
1781

WASHINGTON and ROCHAMBEAU

BRITISH SQUADRON

Chesapeake Bay

Yorktown

CORNWALLIS

DE GRASSE

calmly listen to threatenings of slaughter against them. Were a people spreading desolation with fire and sword in England, I, as an inhabitant, whether the invaders were right or wrong, would probably feel as the Americans now do, and use the same harsh expressions: thus I reason, and cannot therefore condemn—but the grace of God is sufficient to set us all above the world, and all things here.

1781 *Sunday, October 21. I attended the Episcopal church twice. Our own house was crowded. The work of God appears still to revive amongst us; and I trust the*

fidelity required by the act of the State of Maryland, was preposterously rigid.

Tuesday, June 6. I keep up prayer in public or private twelve times a day; and am exercised not a little. Lord, keep me through the approaching troubles of the continent!

Friday, September 8. I have a natural affection for my own countrymen; yet I can hear them called cruel people, and

WASHINGTON'S ENTRY INTO NEW YORK
ON THE EVACUATION OF THE BRITISH,
NOVEMBER 25, 1783

society increases in grace as well as in numbers. Among too many of the citizens the spirit of politics has, in whole or in part, eaten out the spirit of religion.

1783 *Saturday, April 5. I heard the news that peace was confirmed between England and America. I had various exercises of mind on the occasion: it may cause great changes to take place amongst us; some for the better, and some for the worse. It may make against the work of God: our preachers will be far more likely to settle in the world; and our people, by getting into trade, and acquiring wealth, may drink into its spirit.*

FREEBORN GARRETTSON PREACHING IN
DORCHESTER COUNTY JAIL, MARYLAND

THE CHRISTMAS CONFERENCE

The Treaty of Paris severed America from England. This political break also rendered the organization of American Methodism untenable. Embued with a spirit of independence, the American Methodists were in no mood to remain subservient to the national Church of England.

In response to American appeals, Wesley urged the Bishop of London to ordain some of his American preachers. Failing in this, he was driven to that decision he had so long resisted. On September 2, 1784, Wesley, acting without episcopal approval ordained two men and set Dr. Thomas Coke aside to be a superintendent in America. He then commissioned Coke to cross the Atlantic and ordain Francis Asbury as a second superintendent.

In November Coke met Asbury at Barratt's Chapel and informed him of Wesley's plan. Asbury was agreeable, but only on the condition that the American preachers themselves elect him to the high office. They decided to call a conference of itinerants. On a moment's notice, Freeborn Garrettson set out on horseback to spread the news of the conference.

On Christmas Eve, some sixty preachers gathered at Lovely Lane Chapel, Baltimore. During the ensuing week, they established the Methodist Episcopal Church, elected and consecrated Francis Asbury as their superintendent, and agreed on a working constitution of the infant church. On January 1, Asbury left Baltimore to commence his initial tour as bishop of the first distinctly American denomination.

THOMAS COKE

STRAWBERRY ALLEY, FIRST METHODIST MEETINGHOUSE IN BALTIMORE

1784 *Sunday, November 14. I came to Barratt's Chapel: here, to my great joy, I met these dear men of God, Dr. Coke and Richard Whatcoat; we were greatly comforted together. The Doctor preached on "Christ our Wisdom, righteousness, sanctification, and redemption." Having had no opportunity of conversing with them before public worship, I was greatly surprised to see brother Whatcoat assist by taking the cup in the administration of the sacrament. I was shocked when first informed of the intention of these my brethren in coming to this country: it may be of God. My answer then was, if the preachers unanimously choose me, I shall not act in the capacity I have hitherto done by Mr. Wesley's appointment. The design of organizing the Methodists into an Independent Episcopal Church was opened to the preachers present, and it was agreed to call a general conference, to meet at Baltimore the ensuing Christmas; as also that brother Garrettson go off to Virginia to give notice thereof to our brethren in the South.*

FREEBORN GARRETTSON—THE PAUL REVERE
OF METHODISM

way. My soul waits upon God. O that he may lead us in the way we should go! Part of my time is, and must necessarily be, taken up with preparing for the conference.

Tuesday, December 14. I met Dr. Coke at Abingdon, Mr. Richard Dallam kindly taking him there in his coach; he preached on, "He that hath the Son hath life." We talked of our concerns in great love.

Wednesday, 15. My soul was much

blest at the communion, where I believe all were more or less engaged with God. I feel it necessary daily to give up my own will. The Dr. preached a great sermon on, "He that loveth father or mother more than me."

Saturday, 18. Spent the day at Perry Hall, partly in preparing for the conference. My intervals of time I passed in reading the third volume of the British Arminian Magazine. Continued at Perry Hall until *Friday*, the twenty-fourth.

Tuesday, November 16. Rode to Bohemia Manor where I met with Thomas Vasey, who came over with the Doctor and Richard Whatcoat. My soul is deeply engaged with God to know his will in this new business.

Friday, November 26. I observed this day as a day of fasting and prayer, that I might know the will of God in the matter that is shortly to come before our conference: the preachers and people seem to be much pleased with the projected plan; I myself am led to think it is of the Lord. I am not tickled with the honour to be gained—I see danger in the

PERRY HALL—WHERE THE CHRISTMAS CONFERENCE AGENDA WAS PLANNED

A CHURCH IS BORN

We then rode to Baltimore, where we met a few preachers: it was agreed to form ourselves into an Episcopal Church, and to have superintendents, elders, and deacons. When the conference was seated, Dr. Coke and myself were unanimously elected to the superintendency of the Church, and my ordination followed, after being previously ordained deacon and elder. . . .

LOVELY LANE MEETINGHOUSE, 1774-1786

RICHARD WHATCOAT   THOMAS VASEY

Twelve elders were elected, and solemnly set apart to serve our societies in the United States, one for Antigua, and two for Nova Scotia. We spent the whole week in conference, debating freely, and determining all things by a majority of votes. The Doctor preached every day at noon, and some one of the other preachers morning and evening. We were in great haste, and did much business in a little time.

John Wesley to the American brethren
Bristol, September 10, 1784

"I have accordingly appointed Dr. Coke and Mr. Francis Asbury to be joint superintendents over our brethren in North America; as also Richard Whatcoat and Thomas Vasey to act as elders among them, by baptizing and administering the Lord's Supper."

THE CONSECRATION OF BISHOP ASBURY

THE GENESIS OF A NATION—

A WOOD CUT OF OLD GLORY
WITH THIRTEEN STARS

Even before the guns fell silent, the Revolution produced fundamental changes in American society. The Declaration of '76 abruptly ended a century and a half of colonial subservience and gave legitimacy to the ideals of democracy and egalitarianism. Acting with dispatch and bravery, the newly independent states replaced their colonial charters with democratically approved constitutions. Meanwhile, in 1777 members of the War Congress drafted and sent to the states for ratification a national constitution. Four years and several compromises later, all thirteen states consented to the document. The Articles of Confederation officially became the first constitution of the land.

With the aid of French troops and pro-American anti-war protestors in England, the Americans broke the odds and won political recognition. Even still, at the time of the signing of the Treaty of Paris (1783) the United States of America was more a name than a nation. In truth, the Articles (dubbed by critics the Articles of Confusion) provided little more than a loose league of thirteen sovereign states. Without power to regulate trade, or even to tax, the national government was no match for the independently-minded state assemblies which coined their own monies, raised their own armies, and erected tariffs against even their sister states.

By 1786, both the economy and foreign policy of the fledgling nation were in disarray. Equally disturbing to Americans of wealth was the groundswell of support for impoverished debtors like Daniel Shays who took up arms in protest against sound money, high taxes, and home mortgage foreclosures. Though Shays Rebellion was crushed (1787), the outbreak struck fear in the minds of propertied men who wondered if the Revolution had gone too far, and had raised up the monster "Mobocracy," a tyrant they perceived even more dangerous than George III.

A 1786 meeting in Annapolis made little headway in solving the nation's economic crisis, but this Annapolis convention did endorse Alexander Hamilton's proposal to hold a national convention the ensuing year. In response to the request, Congress issued a call for a convention "for the sole and express purpose of revising" the Articles.

In May 1787, twelve states sent delegates to the Philadelphia gathering. Only tiny Rhode Island refused to participate. For seventeen weeks fifty-five delegates met behind closed doors, debating and supposedly revising the Articles. But on September 17, they stunned Congress and the nation when they released their results. Instead of restructuring the existing Articles, the delegates on their own initiative prepared an entirely new constitution and announced it would supercede the Articles when ratified by nine of the thirteen states.

The battle for ratification was intense. Many feared the new constitution created an anti-democratic central government which swallowed both the sovereignty of the states and freedoms of the individuals. Others insisted that without it the nation would crumble into ruins. In the end, the Federalists (pro-constitution advocates) won narrow majorities in the states. By the end of June 1788, the constitution was ratified by the ninth state, New Hampshire, and officially was adopted as the highest law of the land. Out of the pangs of Revolution and counter-Revolution, a "more perfect union" was born.

POPULATION BY REGION: 1790 TO 1810			
	1790	1800	1810
New England	1,009,408	1,233,011	1,471,973
Middle Atlantic	958,632	1,402,565	2,014,702
East No. Central	——	51,006	272,324
West No. Central	——	——	19,783
South Atlantic	1,851,806	2,286,494	2,674,891
East So. Central	109,368	335,407	708,590
West So. Central	——	——	77,618

TOWARDS A "MORE PERFECT UNION"

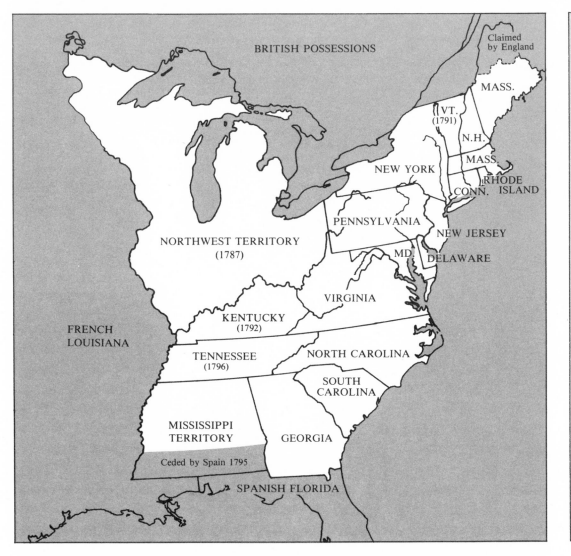

BRITISH POSSESSIONS

Claimed by England

MASS.

VT. (1791)

N.H.

MASS.

NEW YORK

RHODE ISLAND

CONN.

PENNSYLVANIA

NEW JERSEY

NORTHWEST TERRITORY (1787)

MD. DELAWARE

VIRGINIA

KENTUCKY (1792)

FRENCH LOUISIANA

TENNESSEE (1796)

NORTH CAROLINA

SOUTH CAROLINA

MISSISSIPPI TERRITORY

GEORGIA

Ceded by Spain 1795

SPANISH FLORIDA

HISTORICAL PERSPECTIVES

1777 — Delegates to the 2nd Continental Congress draft the Articles of Confederation.

1781 — After being ratified by all thirteen states, the Articles of Confederation becomes the first constitution of the United States.

1783 — England recognizes the independence of America.

1786 — Rising dissatisfaction with the Articles provokes Congress to call for a national convention to amend the constitution.

1787 — Fifty-five delegates from twleve states meet in Philadelphia to revise the Articles. Instead, they discard the old constitution, draft a new one, and send it to the states for ratification.

1788 — New Hampshire becomes the ninth state to ratify the U.S. Constitution, thereby establishing the new government.

1789 — Newly elected George Washington takes the presidential oath on a crowded balcony overlooking Wall Street, New York City.

1790 — First U.S. Census taken.

1791 — The Bill of Rights is added to the constitution.

TRAVELS ACROSS NEW ENGLAND—

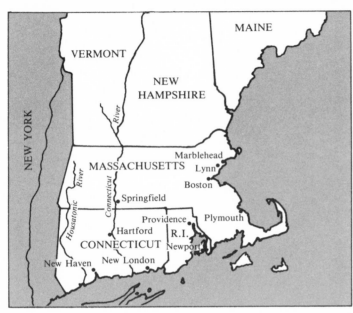

Throughout the colonial era—from the arrival of the Pilgrims in 1620 to the spirited "great awakenings" under Jonathan Edwards and George Whitefield well over a hundred years later—New England stood as a "city on a hill." At least among Americans, it was a region renowned for religious fervor and vitality. Unfortunately for Methodists, however, the strong Calvinistic orientation of the region, as well as the blatant anti-British sentiments of New England patriots, curtailed the work of Wesleyan missionaries. In comparison with other areas on the American continent, New England for many years was barren ground for Methodistic Christianity.

If slow germinating, the seeds of New England Methodism eventually did take root. The miniscule 181-member, three-circuit field of 1790 sprouted within thirty years into a religiously fertile domain which included nearly 18,000 members and seventy-four circuits. Hence, despite Asbury's grumblings about the mercantile spirit of New Englanders, and about their unsavory appetite for extravagant steeples financed by renting out church pews, by the time of the bishop's death, the land of John Winthrop was on its way towards becoming the land of John Wesley as well.

1791

Saturday, June 4. I rode over rocks and hills, and came to Wilton; and preached to a serious, feeling, well-behaved people at Squire Rockwell's. In the evening I went on to Redding. Surely God will work powerfully amongst these people, and save thousands of them. We have travelled about twenty-four miles this day over very rough roads; the weather is cold for the season; my horse is very small, and my carriage is inconvenient in such rocky, uneven, jolting ways. This country is very hilly and open—not unlike that about the Peak of Derbyshire. I feel faith to believe that this visit to New England will be blessed to my own soul, and the souls of others. We are now in Connecticut; and never out of sight of a house; and sometimes we have a view of many churches and steeples, built very neatly of wood; either for use, ornament, piety, policy, or interest—or it may be some of all these.

FIRST METHODIST PREACHING HOUSE
IN BOSTON, 1795

CONNECTICUT

Friday, June 10. From New Haven, through a poor country, we passed on to Northbury, where there is a large Independent Church. In Wallingford the meetinghouse of the Separatists supplied a place for our preachers; we have also used a neat Episcopal church—small indeed, compared to others.

I am reminded of England in travelling here; this country more resembles my own than any I have yet seen on this side of the Atlantic.

A TYPICAL NEW ENGLAND TOWN, WINDHAM, CONN.

NEW ENGLAND WOMEN

1794 *Tuesday, August 5. We passed Windham and Mansfield. We were met by a powerful thundergust; but stepping into a house, escaped its effects: this is one advantage which we have in travelling in the eastern, rather than the western country; in the latter, oftentimes there is not a house for miles—in the former there are houses always in sight.*

1800 *Friday, July 11. The simplicity and frugality of New England is desirable—you see the woman a mother, mistress, maid, and wife, and in all these characters a conversable woman; she seeth to her own house, parlour, kitchen and dairy. . . . If you wish breakfast at six or seven o'clock there is no setting the table an hour before the provision can be produced.*

MOUNT TOM, AND CONNECTICUT RIVER

NEW HAVEN

according to my reckoning, travelled five thousand miles: everlasting glory be to my all sufficient God!

1809 *May 23. On Tuesday I came to Peck's, Stratford, and thence on to father Jocelin's, New Haven, weary, and sleepy, and glad to rest. I dined with W. Griffin in Guildford: here is a lot to build a house of worship on, and God will work here. In the afternoon I preached at Jeremiah Miner's, in Killingworth; thence crossing the Connecticut River, came into New London. . . . I gave them a discourse on 1 John ii, 6. The house was soon filled, and many went away who could not get in.*

1804 *Sabbath Day, June 24. O, New Haven! Thou seat of science and sin! Can thy dry bones live? Lord, thou knowest!*

1805 *Tuesday, June 25. At the Square Ponds meetinghouse I preached upon Rom. viii, 1,2. It was an open season—the best time I have had in New England. Several felt. I hope it is a prelude to a revival here. I am resting, writing, and reading our Form of Discipline, and the Jews' Answer to Voltaire.*

1806 *Sunday, May 25. I preached at New Haven. . . . Since the 16th of April, 1805, I have,*

YALE COLLEGE, NEW HAVEN, CONN.

TRAVELS ALONG THE HOUSATONIC RIVER

1813
Saturday, June 26. Came the Hartford Bridge road to Jonathan Coe's, Winstead. Hail, home! Rest, my heart! We have made a stand in the New England Conference against steeples and pews; and shall possibly give up the houses, unless the pews are taken out, and the houses made sure to us exclusively. The conference now pursues a course which will surely lead to something decisive: we will be flattered no longer.

HISTORICAL PERSPECTIVES ON NEW ENGLAND

1620 — Pilgrims aboard the Mayflower land near Plymouth Rock.

1636 — Harvard College established to train colonial ministers.

1692 — Salem Village holds witchcraft trials.

1741 — George Whitfield preaches farewell sermon before 16,000 hearers at the Boston Commons.

1772 — Relations with England strained when patriots destroy a British patrol ship, the *Gaspee*, off the coast of Rhode Island.

1775 — Battle of Bunker Hill.

1777 — Vermont emancipates its slaves.

1786 — Phillis Wheatley, black American poet, publishes her first work in America.

1791 — Jesse Lee establishes the first Methodist society in Massachusetts.

1814 — New England Federalists dissatisfied with President Madison's handling of the War of 1812 meet in Hartford, Connecticut, to discuss possible secession from the Union.

1791 *Saturday, June 25. I preached at Slade's Tavern* on my way to Lynn, on "If our Gospel be hid, it is hid to them that are lost." I was agreeably surprised to find a house raised for the Methodists. As a town, I think Lynn the perfection of beauty; it is seated on a plain, under a range of craggy hills, and open to the sea: there is a promising society—an exceedingly well-behaved congregation—these things, doubtless, made all pleasing to me. My first subject was Rom. viii, 33, in the afternoon Acts iv, 12: here we shall make a firm stand, and from this central point, from Lynn, shall the light of Methodism and of truth radiate through the State.

1795 *Monday, July 27. Since I have been in Lynn, I have* visited Wood End and Gravesend, met five classes, visited about one dozen families, and talked to them personally about their souls, and prayed with them. I have filled up intervals in reading my Bible, and the second volume of Mr. Wesley's Sermons.

Monday, August 10. I stopped, and gave an exhortation at Springfield. After a thundergust, we came on to Agawam. If I accomplish the tour I have in contemplation, it will make about six or seven hundred miles to the city of New York. I was stopped by the rain; but when I cannot do one thing, another offers. I could read, write, pray, and plan. I laid out a plan for my travels in 1797; through Connecticut, Rhode Island, Massachusetts, Province of

BENJAMIN JOHNSON HOUSE, LYNN, MASS.
LEE PREACHED HERE IN DECEMBER, 1790.
ON FEBRUARY 20, 1791, HE FORMED IN LYNN
THE FIRST METHODIST CHURCH IN THE STATE
WITH EIGHT MEMBERS.

S.W. VIEW OF THE STATEHOUSE IN BOSTON

Maine, New Hampshire, Vermont, and New York: making a distance of twelve or fifteen hundred miles.

1800 *Tuesday, July 15. We came through Wrentham,* Walpole, Dedham, and Roxbury to Boston: it was a damp day, with an easterly wind, unfriendly to my breast. As they were about finishing our church we could not preach in it. The new Statehouse here is, perhaps, one of the most simply elegant in the United States.

NEWBURYPORT MARBLEHEAD SPRINGFIELD

Friday, July 25. We rode through Weston, where is a grand steeple, porches, and even stalls for the horses; and it is well if they do not make the Methodists pay to support their pomp. O! religion in New England!

1802 *Thursday, June 24. We reached Marblehead. Brother Whatcoat preached; I have an exhortation: our audience, chiefly females, nearly filled the room.*

Friday, 25. We rode round the tomb of that old prophet of the Lord, George Whitefield. We stopped at the sisters Eaton's, in Salisbury, and allow ourselves to have made six hundred and twenty miles. In Newburyport are great

HARVARD COLLEGE

improvements, and beautiful houses in and around: as in Boston, everything thrives but religion.

Friday, July 9. Haverhill bridge engaged my attention. It is thrown across the Merrimack River by three arches; a distance of probably sixteen hundred feet. I also saw the grand canal, designed, principally, to float lumber from the Merrimack to Boston. For about twenty-seven miles they have rocks, and swamps, and hills to wind and labour through; nevertheless, they can draw a raft of great length along, after passing the locks, which admit about seventy feet at a time; they link the disparted fragments together again, and move forward. This navigation will be a vast source of wealth to the country.

THE OLD SOUTH PRESBYTERIAN
CHURCH, NEWBURYPORT, MASS.

BANKS OF THE HOUSATONIC, AT PITTSFIELD

1804 _Wednesday, July 25._ At Greenfield, in Massachusetts, we breakfasted, having passed Barnardston, the first village we entered in the State. We started away again to Deerfield, and Conway, and Ashville, and Plainfield, and Commington, and Windsor, and Dalton, and Pittsfield, and Richmond, and so out of the State; but I was glad to stop fifteen miles short of Pittsfield, after riding over dreadful hills and rocks forty-five miles: we took our breakfast with Robert Green, in Pittsfield. Here we crossed the head branch of the Housatonic River.

1812 _Sunday, June 28._ There is a serious division in Pittsfield—about thirty members have withdrawn. They have built a neat house in Lynn; but I am afraid of a steeple; and if they put this foolish addition, it must not be by Methodist order, or with Methodist money—they may pay for their own pride and folly. We had great peace and order in the New England Conference; but we are poor.

1803 _Monday, June 13._ I will not mention names, but I could tell of a congregation that sold their priest to another congregation in Boston for the sum of one thousand dollars, and hired out the money at the unlawful interest of twenty-five or thirty percent. Lord, have mercy upon the priest and people that can think of buying the kingdom of heaven with money!

''Poor New England! She is the Valley of dry bones still! Come, O breath of the Lord, and breathe upon these slain that they may live!''

Journals, June 4, 1803

RHODE ISLAND

1791 _Sunday, June 19._ Came to Providence.

Monday, 20. I visited some serious families that truly love and fear God. . . . The people here appear to be prudent, active, frugal—cultivating a spirit of good family economy; and they are kind to strangers. They have had frequent revivals of religion: I had faith to believe the Lord would shortly visit them again, and that even we shall have something to do in this town.

1798 _Tuesday, July 31._ We came upon Rhode Island; stopped at Matthew Cook's, dined, and then came to our little meetinghouse, and had a good season on Heb. x, 38, 39. This island is most beautiful in its situation

SLATER MILL, PAWTUCKET, R.I., ca. 1810

INDIAN ROCK—NARRAGANSETT, R.I.

and cultivation; the neat stone square walls, level fields of grass, corn, and barley, sloping to the water, are very pleasing to the eye: salt water prospects are most delightful. Upon the summits of the island you may see from water to water. Here fruit trees, fish, and shell fish abound. The Friends meetinghouse is large, and the settlement extensive; and if the Baptists, Moravians, Episcopalians, Friends, and Methodists have any religion, there must be some good people here. Rhode Island is by far the most beautiful island I have seen.

1809 _May 26._ We crossed Narragansett Bay on _Friday_, and came into Newport. Grand house; steeple, pews; by lottery: the end is to sanctify the means; Ah! What pliability to evil!

Sabbath, 28. I preached twice; in the forenoon on Col. ii, 1, 2; 1 John iii, 3-5, in the afternoon. I spoke with difficulty and with little order in my discourses. From New York thus far we have had dust and rough roads, and I have been much tried and greatly blessed. We have ridden two hundred miles in six days.

NEW HAMPSHIRE

VERMONT

1802 *Friday, July 9. I crossed New Hampshire from Saybrook to Berwick, a distance of thirty miles, and recrossed from Berwick to Plaistow, a distance of forty miles. The native products of the soil are the spruce, pine, cedar, birch, oak, ash—it is a rich lumber country, well watered, with fine streams for saw mills. The face of the earth is not pleasing, but it is well improved: the prospects for Indian corn are good, the clover fields luxuriant, and the meadows beautiful: the dwellings are handsome, and the meetinghouses stand within sight of each other.*

LEMUEL HAYNEW—FIRST BLACK MINISTER OF THE CONGREGATIONAL CHURCH IN AMERICA

A NEW ENGLAND LUMBER MILL

1803 *Tuesday, June 21. Next day we crossed the Connecticut River at Barrett's Ferry, and came into the city of Brattleboro, stopping at Joseph Jacob's. We are now in Vermont. The stupendous steeps on each side of the river resemble those at Harper's Ferry, and the precipitous heights of the North River. . . . My mind enjoys great calm; and I have faith to believe that as God is working gloriously in other parts of the continent, He will make a display of his power even here, and bid the dry bones live.*

ISLES OF SHOALS, NEW HAMPSHIRE

MAINE AND BEYOND

1802 *Tuesday, June 29.* We stopped at Falmouth in the District of Maine; and within sight of Portland. Although we rode thirty miles I was obliged to preach—my subject was 2 Tim. iv, 7.

Thursday, July 1. Our conference continued three days. We held it in the upper room of Sewell Prescott's house. We had fifteen members, and nine probationers: the married preachers who came deficient to our conference received about one hundred and twenty dollars; the single brethren about sixty-two dollars; and the probationers a small donation of two dollars each, which came from afar.

1811 *Tuesday, July 2.* We rode through Cornwall [Canada] in the night, and came to Evan Roy's making forty-four miles for the day's journey. It is surprising how we make nearly fifty miles a day over such desperate roads as we have lately travelled; we lose no time: Ah! why should we—it is so precious! My strong affection for the people of the United States came with strange power upon me while I was crossing the line. . . . Thursday, on the opposite shore they are firing for the Fourth of July. What have I to do with this waste of powder? I pass the pageantry of day unheeded on the other side: why should I have new feelings in Canada?

READFIELD MEETINGHOUSE—THE FIRST METHODIST CHURCH IN MAINE, 1795

ALONG THE COAST OF MAINE

METHODIST EXPANSION IN NEW ENGLAND	
1790 —	781
1800 —	5,838
1810 —	11,220
1820 —	17,739

NEW YORK and NEW JERSEY

ST. PAUL'S EPISCOPAL
CHURCH, NEW YORK

Sailing in 1609 for the Dutch East Indian Company, English born Henry Hudson explored the North American coast in search for the elusive (and non-existent) northwest passage to the Orient. Though failing in his mission, Hudson discovered a deep water bay and river, named them after himself, and claimed for Holland the forested land of New Netherlands.

Life in New Netherlands was harsh. Established by and for a corporation with only profit making in mind, the Dutch Colony offered its inhabitants few civil or religious liberties. Dissenters received swift and often brutal punishment. By mid-century, New Netherlands could boast of a large (10,000 strong) population, but certainly not a loyal one.

The days of Dutch control of the region were numbered. In 1664, Charles II of England awarded the area to his brother James, the Duke of York, and promptly sent a squadron of English ships to claim it by force. But when the soldiers arrived, the Dutch settlers treated them more as liberators than invaders. Without having to fire a shot, overnight New Netherlands became New York.

Jubilant over the victory, James granted a portion of his newly acquired territory to a group of English courtiers. Within fifteen years, however, the proprietors of Jersey sold their interest to a body of Quakers who turned the colony into a sanctuary for persecuted Friends. New York, on the other hand, became a Royal Colony in 1684 when the death of Charles II placed the Duke of York, James II, on the English throne.

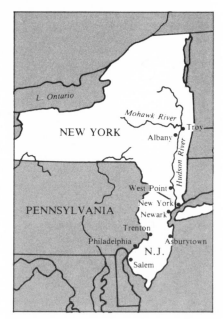

FEDERAL HALL, U.S. CAPITOL, 1789-1790

1784 *Friday, August 27. We had a trying journey to New York; the weather being excessively warm. I found my old friends John Chave and William Lupton at Newark, who appeared pleased to see me. We took the stage, and reached New York about eight o'clock. At New York we found the people alive to God: there are about one hundred in society, and, with those in Philadelphia, to my mind, appear more like Methodists than I have ever yet seen them. My first discourse was for the benefit of poor stragglers, who have not yet returned to the fold: the subject chosen was Rev. iii, 1-4.*

1786

I reached New York on the thirty-first of August, having travelled three hundred and fifty miles since I left Bath, in Virginia. I was taken ill, and was confined about eight days, during which time I was variously tried and exercised in mind. I spent some time in looking over my journals, which I have kept for fifteen years back. Some things I corrected, and some I expunged. Perhaps, if they are not published before, they will be after my death, to let my friends and the world see how I have employed my time in America. I feel the worth of souls, and the weight of the pastoral charge, and that the conscientious discharge of its important duties requires something more than human learning, unwieldy salaries, or clerical titles of D.D., or even bishop. The eyes of all—both preachers and people, will be opened in time.

1787

Tuesday, May 22. Rode twenty miles on Long Island, to Hempstead Harbour, and preached with some liberty in the evening. I am now out of the city, and have time to reflect: my soul turns to its rest, and to its labour for souls, in which I can live more by rule.

Sunday, 27. I came to Harper's, where we have a little new house, and about thirty members: I hope, and expect, in a few years, to see a circuit of six weeks formed here, and four or five hundred members in society. The people on this island, who hear the Gospel, are generally poor, and these are the kind I want, and expect to get.

Wednesday, June 6. Met leaders and trustees and after some explanation, settled matters relative to singing in public worship. I preached at the poorhouse on "Whosoever shall call on the name of the Lord shall be saved."

STAGE FOR NEW YORK

Saturday, June 16. Rode over the mountains, and was gratified with the sight of a remarkable recess for the Americans during the last war: the names of Andre and Arnold, with which misfortune and treachery are so unhappily and intimately blended, will give celebrity to West Point, had it been less deserving of notice than its wonderful appearance really makes it. It is commanded by mountains rising behind, and appears to be impregnable: there are blockhouses on the east; and on the west, stores, barracks, and fortifications. From West Point we crossed a high mountain, and came to Newburg.

1789 Friday, June 19. I preached in a barn on the North River: my hearers were chiefly Low Dutch. Our congregations are small; the craft is in danger; we are therefore not to wonder if we meet with opposition. To begin at the right end of the work is to go first to the poor, these will, the rich may possibly, hear the truth.

1791 Thursday, May 26. Our conference came together in great peace and love. . . . Nothing

ENTRANCE TO THE HUDSON HIGHLANDS, NEAR NEWBURGH

would satisfy the conference and the society but my consenting to preach on the occasion of Mr. Wesley's death, which I did on Sunday, May 29: my text was 2 Tim. iii, 10, 11.

1793 Friday, July 19. We hope two hundred souls have been awakened, and as many converted in Albany district the past year. Our friends are happy here, not being distressed with divisions in the Church,

nor by war with the Indians, as they are to the southward. According to our reckoning, we make it about four hundred and forty-seven miles from Old Town to Albany—to come the mountainous road through the woods; and to come by Baltimore, Philadelphia, and New York, it is six hundred miles.

Thursday, August 22. Came to New York. The weather is extremely warm. Great afflictions prevail here—fluxes, fevers, influenzas. It is very sickly also in Philadelphia. I have found by secret search, that I have not preached sanctification as I should have done: if I am restored, this shall be my theme more pointedly than ever, God being my helper.

1796 Monday, August 15. We rode to New York: whilst crossing the ferry some foolish, wicked people uttered so many _damns_, that I was a little afraid the Lord would sink the boat: I asked a man if he had any chalk to lend me that I might mark down the curses the company gave us on our passage of thirty or forty minutes.

A VIEW OF WEST POINT, NEW YORK

NEW YORK CITY, ca. 1800

1803 <u>Monday, July 11</u>. I have travelled about two hundred miles through the State of New York. By a fair and accurate computation I judge that we have added, exclusive of the dead, the removed, and the expelled, and withdrawn, 17,300: Our total for the year 1803 is 104,070 members: in 1771 there were about 300 Methodists in New York, 250 in Philadelphia, and a few in Jersey; I then longed for 100,000; now I want 200,000—nay, thousands upon thousands.

1805 <u>Wednesday, May 22</u>. In this State the subjects of succession, rebaptizing, are much agitated. I will tell the world what I rest my authority upon.
1. Divine authority.
2. Seniority in America. 3. The election of the General Conference.
4. My ordination by Thomas Coke, William Phillip Otterbein, German Presbyterian minister, Richard Whatcoat, and Thomas Vasey.
5. Because the signs of an apostle have been seen in me.

THE FALLS AT CATSKILL

1802 <u>Monday, June 7</u>. How sweet to me are all the moving and still life scenes which now surround me on every side! The quiet country houses; the fields and orchards, bearing the promise of the fruitful year; the flocks and herds, the hills and vales, and dewey meads; the gliding streams and murmuring brooks: and thou, too, solitude—with thy attendants, silence and meditation—how dost thou solace my pensive mind after the tempest of fear, and care, and tumult, and talk, experienced in the noisy, bustling city!

1807 _Thursday, July 2._ We dined at Geneva, on Seneca Lake: the lake is about forty miles in length, and from one to five miles wide. . . . This is a great land for wheat, rye, and grass; and the lakes, with their navigation of vessels and boats, and moving scenes, make the prospects beautiful.

1810 _Friday, July 6._ Our ease in Zion makes me feel awful: who shall reform the reformers? Ah, poor dead Methodists! I have seen preachers' children wearing gold— brought up in pride. Ah, mercy, mercy!

Monday, 9. We bent our way up to Catskill, and crossed the mountains to Middlesburg. Some foolish boys were at cards; we were, however, respectfully treated. I prayed heartily for the family, and gave away some good books, and blessed the household in the name of the Holy Trinity: shall our blessing be lost? We directed our course towards the New Sharon camp meeting. I know not if the people might not starve in the mountains, were it not for the sawmills and lumber.

"My attention was strongly excited by the steamboat: this is a great invention."

Journals, May 5, 1809

TRAVELING THROUGH JERSEY

COURTHOUSE AT SALEM, N.J.—SITE FOR EARLY
METHODIST PREACHING

1785 *Saturday, September 24.
Preached at Salem and at
Stow Creek, with some consolation:
many attended although it rained, and
we had a comfortable time at sacrament.
I plunged H.T. and S.M. in Salem
Creek: this unusual baptismal ceremony
might, perhaps, have made our congrega-*

*tion larger than it would otherwise have
been. Lord, help me to keep on, under
all my troubles of body and mind!*

1791 *Sunday, May 22. I
preached in Trenton, on
Joel ii, 17. Several preachers exhorted,
and the Lord made sinners tremble.
Eighteen years ago I often slipped away
from Philadelphia to Burlington one
week, and to Trenton another, to keep a
few souls alive: I had then no conferences to take up my time and occupy
my thoughts; and now—what hath God
wrought!*

1795 *Monday, September 28.
We came to Monmouth.
. . . I was shocked at the brutality of
some men who were fighting; one gouged
out the other's eye; the father and son
then beset him again, cut off his ears
and nose, and beat him almost to death.
The father and son were tried for a
breach of the peace, and roundly fined;
and now the man that hath lost his nose
and ears is to come upon them for
damage. I have often thought that there*

NEW JERSEY FARMER, 1790s

*are some things practiced in the Jerseys
which are more brutish and diabolical
than in any of the other states: there is
nothing of this kind in New England;
they learn civility there at least.*

1806 *Monday, May 5. I
preached at Elizabethtown,
and then came on to Newark. . . . We
have a warm day, the harbinger of
spring: universal nature seems starting
innumerable forms of promise of the
fruitful year—O that it may be so
spiritually!*

A VIEW OF TRENTON, N.J., ca. 1800

HISTORICAL PERSPECTIVES ON THE MID-ATLANTIC STATES

1609 — Henry Hudson claims the Hudson River Valley for the Dutch.

1664 — Charles II gives the Duke of York a land grant between Maryland and New England.

1681 — William Penn receives a grant from the king to settle Pennsylvania.

1704 — The Anglican Church is established in New Jersey.

1776 — The population of Philadelphia reaches 40,000.

1787 — Delaware ratifies the new constitution, thus becoming the first state in the Union.

1804 — Republican Vice-President Aaron Burr kills Federalist Alexander Hamilton in a duel near Weekauken, New Jersey.

1807 — Robert Fulton develops the first practical steamboat.

1816 — The African Methodist Episcopal Church is organized in Philadelphia.

Thursday, May 9. We came to Asbury, and I preached and added a special exhortation. Were it not for the brewing and drinking miserable whiskey, Asburytown would be a pleasant place. Friday, to James Egbert's. Bethel chapel has been bought and refitted for the Methodists: I preached in it. I am unknown in Jersey and ever shall be, I presume: after forty years' labour we have not ten thousand in membership.

PENNSYLVANIA and DELAWARE

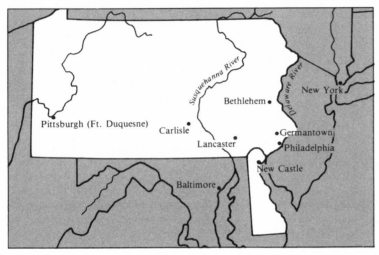

Beginning in the 1660's a devout group of English dissenters, commonly known as the Quakers, challenged the authorities of both the church and the state. This remarkable religious group, formally called the Society of Friends, refused to support the Church of England with taxes, take oaths, or serve in the military. Like the Puritans of fifty years earlier and the Methodists of seventy years later, the Quakers faced severe persecution from state officials. Thousands were imprisoned for remaining true to their peculiar beliefs.

Though hardly sympathetic to their religion, in 1681 King Charles II became the Friends "best friend." Making good on an old debt, Charles repaid the Quaker son of Admiral Sir William Penn with a fertile tract of land in the New World. Charles named the land, Pennsylvania—literally, Penn's Woodlands.

Young William established his colony as a haven for persecuted Quakers. It also was intended as a model for Christian living, a "holy experiment." With liberal laws, no tax-supported church, freedom of worship for all religious bodies, and no provision for a military defense, Pennsylvania was a noble experiment which attracted a richly mixed racial group. Within twenty years—by 1700—Pennsylvania already had surpassed all the colonies in population with the exceptions of long established Virginia and Massachusetts. Penn's beautiful forest was a modern enterprise in an unmodern age.

1785 *Sunday, September 25. Next morning we came to Cooper's Ferry, and although the wind blew violently in the morning, when we came to the ferry all was calm. We breakfasted in Philadelphia early enough for church.*

1787 *Tuesday, September 25. I attended at Chester; and next day came to Philadelphia. I had liberty in speaking on Cant. v, 6-10. On Thursday and Friday, I had not freedom as I wished. I was seized with a violent headache, exceeding anything, as I thought, I had ever felt.*

Saturday, 29. I felt a little better. My mind was stayed upon God.

1789 *Friday, July 3. Came to Philadelphia: here I found enough to do. My soul longs for more religion in this city; I am distressed for these people: twenty years have we been labouring in Pennsylvania, and there not one thousand in society: how many of these are truly converted, God knows.*

CHRIST CHURCH, PHILADELPHIA

Friday, July 10. We came to York; but I felt no desire to preach. I proceeded on to Carlisle; in the morning I was permitted to preach in the church; but in the evening, this privilege was denied me: it was said, the reason was, because I did not read prayers, which I had forborne to do because of my eyes; I apprehend the true cause might be found in the pointed manner in which I spoke on "Blessed is he whosoever shall not be offended in me." I went to the courthouse and called them to repentance, from "Look unto me, and be ye saved, all ye ends of the earth"; to the great offence of all who set themselves up for judges, and who declared it was no preaching.

Wednesday, 15. Came to Juniata River; we were well nigh being lost in the woods, but kind Providence brought us safe in company with brother Whatcoat to I. C_____'s, and we lodged there.

DESCENT INTO THE VALLEY OF WYOMING

Saturday, July 31. I spoke on education, from Prov. xxii, 6. I was led to enlarge on the obligations of parents to their children; and the nature of that religious education which would be mostly to fit them for this, and which alone could qualify them for the next world.

Monday, September 20. I reached the city of Philadelphia. Our brethren have built a new chapel, thirty feet square, at the south end of the city. I feel myself fatigued and unwell, occasioned by riding a rough-going horse.

Tuesday, 21. This day was spent in reading, writing, and visiting.

Wednesday, 22. The conference began in poor Pennsylvania district: all was peace and love. Our printing is in a good state. Our society in the city of Philadelphia are generally poor: perhaps it is well; when men become rich, they sometimes forget that they are Methodists.

1790
Our conference began at Uniontown on Wednesday the twenty-eighth of July—it was conducted in peace and love. On Thursday I preached.

I am weak, and have been busy, and am not animated by the hope of doing good here. I have therefore been silent the whole week. "I must needs go through Samaria."

PHILADELPHIA—CITY OF BROTHERLY LOVE

Sunday, September 26. Many felt and wept, whilst I enlarged on "The Lord is in his holy temple." At the new chapel, called Ebenezer, in the afternoon, my subject was I Sam. vii, 12. I first explained the text; then showed the Methodist doctrine and discipline, and the work God had wrought by them in this country.

1791 _Tuesday, September 20. Rode to Philadelphia. Here as usual, I was closely employed in writing: I had several meetings, and some awful seasons that will be remembered in eternity. This city abounds with inhabitants—it is the London of America._

OLD EBENEZER, 1790. THE FIRST CHURCH BUILT BY METHODISTS OF PHILADELPHIA.

SHIP BUILDING IN PHILADELPHIA

1792 _Sunday, July 8. I preached at Ebenezer church on James iv, 8; at St. George's church on Mark viii, 38. I had large accounts from the eastward, and am requested to send them more preachers. After twenty years' standing of the house in our hands, the galleries are put up in our old new church._

Monday and Tuesday, 9, 10. Employed in reading and writing. I wish to be alone. O how sweet is solitude!

BANK OF THE UNITED STATES, PHILADELPHIA, ca. 1800

1795 *Sunday, June 21. I preached in the city of Philadelphia three times, not with the success I would wish. I was exceedingly assisted in meeting the classes, in which I spent three days, and am now of opinion that there is more religion among the society than I expected. I trust they and myself will remember this visit for days to come.*

1796 *Monday, August 1. I drew the outlines of a subscription, that may form a part of a constitution of a general fund, for the sole purpose of supporting the travelling ministry; to have respect,*

First, To the single men that suffer and are in want.

Secondly, To the married travelling preachers.

Thirdly, To the worn-out preachers.

Fourthly, The widows and orphans of those who have lived and died in the work. And

Fifthly, To enable the yearly conference to employ more married men; and, finally, to supply the wants of all the travelling preachers, under certain regulations and restrictions as the state of the fund will admit.

EZEKIEL COOPER—FIRST BOOK AGENT
OF THE M.E. CHURCH

Monday, October 10. We opened a conference of between forty and fifty preachers; we had great love and great riches also: never before have we been able to pay the preachers their salaries; at this conference we have done it, and had two hundred dollars left for debts and difficulties the preachers had been involved in.

1799 *Thursday, June 6. We held our conference in Philadelphia. I retired each night to the Eagleworks, upon Schuylkill, at Henry Foxall's solitary, social retreat. The conference was large, and the business*

AN EAST VIEW OF GRAY'S FERRY ON THE RIVER SCHUYLKILL

very important. Ezekiel Cooper was confirmed in his appointment by me as our agent in the book concern.

1803

Monday, July 25. I passed through Lancaster, called upon John Shainer, upon Little Conastoga, dined at Columbia and preached at three o'clock and then crossed the ferry and reached Henry Strickler's to lodge for the night. We stole a march upon our friends at York, and met them at the courthouse as they were coming to meet us.

Friday, 29. We had a sultry ride to Carlisle. Henry Boehm preached in the evening. Next day at eleven o'clock, I gave them a sermon from Col. iii, 12–14: in the evening Wilson Lee spoke.

August 2. On Tuesday morning, at four o'clock, we set out to scale the mountains. We passed a little town called Strasburg, and another called Emmitsburg: here we stopped, and I laid myself down upon the floor to rest; intense heat, rugged mountains, and a wasting dysentery almost overcame me. I feel, and have felt thirty-two years, for Pennsylvania—the most wealthy, and

SOUTHWEST VIEW OF LANCASTER, PA.

''We came off with courage, passing through Lancaster still unpropitious to Methodism: seven miles beyond, Father Musselman received us with a smiling countenance, a willing hand, and ready mind. We fed, and talked, and sang, and prayed, and parted in the Lord.''
                                    Journals, August 12, 1805

the most careless about God, and the things of God: but I hope God will shake the State and the churches. There are now upwards of twenty German preachers somehow connected with Mr. Phillip Otterbein and Martin Boehm; but they want authority, and the Church wants discipline.

BISHOP RICHARD ALLEN—FOUNDER OF
THE A.M.E. CHURCH

1804 *Sunday, May 27. On the Sabbath* we crossed the Susquehanna at M'Call's ferry, and came to Martin Boehm's. I preached at Boehm's chapel, and then came to Soudersburg.

Saturday, June 2. I rode through the rain to the Valley, twenty-eight miles. On the *Sabbath* day, I reached Radnor. Here my little Jane was horned by a cow, and lamed: she is done, perhaps, forever for me; but it may be all for the best. I am unwell, and the weather is bad, but, except my feelings for the poor beast, I am peaceful and resigned.

On *Monday* morning I desired Isaac James to ride thirty miles, going and coming, and purchase me another little Jane, at eighty dollars; he did so, with great good will. I came to Philadelphia, and found that Richard Allen had bought me a horse for ninety dollars; so I had two, one to sell for sixty dollars: so much for my haste.

1807 *Friday, July 17.* To Sutton's ten miles: the house neat as a palace; and we were entertained like kings, by a king and a queen; it was no small consolation to lie down on a clean floor after all we had suffered from dirt and all its consequences. Once more I am at Wyoming. We have wearied through and clambered over one hundred miles of the rough roads of wild Sus-

CROSSING THE SUSQUEHANNA BY FERRY

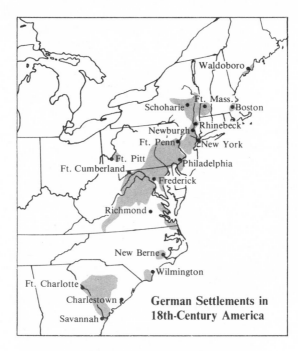

German Settlements in 18th-Century America

THE MORAVIAN VILLAGE OF BETHLEHEM, N.E. PENNSYLVANIA

quehanna. O, the precipitous banks, wedging narrows, rocks, sideling hills, obstructed paths, and fords scarcely fordable, roots, stumps, and gullies!

July 21. We came along, early on Tuesday, through the Wind Gap, seventeen miles to Heller's, and breakfasted. I took a look at the Moravian town of Nazareth; it may contain forty houses built in the German taste and style. . . . The land in the vicinity was not so fertile, nor the grounds as highly improved, as I expected to have found them.

Seventeen miles farther brought us to far-famed Bethlehem, which I had long wished to see. The stream that runs west of the town is pretty and useful, as it works a machine which raises the water one hundred and fifty feet into two reservoirs, for the use of the inhabitants. We found ourselves at the grand tavern at the north end, the property of the brethren: the house is large, but a plain building: the entertainment good at a

dollar a night for man and horse. On the second step of the high grounds on the main street, which begins on the hill above, stand the church buildings. . . . On the same street below stands the brethren's house, one hundred feet front, five stories high, very plain, and much German taste discoverable everywhere; add to this the majestic Lehigh, and you have the most striking features of this celebrated place.

59

COURTHOUSE AT NEW CASTLE, DEL.

1790 *Thursday, October 14. Reached New Castle, in Delaware, and once more preached there, and had a few serious hearers.*

Sunday, 17. We had a gracious love feast, and a very powerful meeting; many bore a living testimony; there was great life and shouting among the people of God.

1800 *Saturday, May 31. I preached at the forest chapel, on Habakkak iii, 2, and rode to Dover that evening.*

Sunday, June 1. This was a day to be remembered: we began our love feast at halfpast eight; meeting was continued (except one hour's intermission) until four o'clock, and some people never left the house until nearly midnight: many souls professed to find the Lord.

DISTANT VIEW OF THE DELAWARE WATER GAP

"In crossing the Delaware we encountered an uncommon storm, but were providentially brought safely over."

Journals, May 21, 1789

MARYLAND and WASHINGTON, D.C.

Though established in 1634 by the Lord Baltimore family as a haven for English Catholics, the Roman influence in Maryland quickly declined as shiploads of English Protestants immigrated to the rich and fertile Chesapeake colony. By the middle decades of the seventeenth century, the transition was complete. The Church of England became the established church in the colony; and Catholic worship, at least in public, was legally forbidden.

In Maryland, as in other thoroughly Anglican colonies, the Methodist movement spread rapidly, especially among the middling classes of society. And despite severe anti-Methodist persecution during the revolutionary years, at the time of the organizational Christmas conference in 1784, more Methodists resided in Maryland than in any of the other newly independent states. Throughout the age of Asbury, Maryland remained a primal center of church activity, with Baltimore the "capital of American Methodism."

ST. MARY'S CITY. THE FIRST PERMANENT SETTLEMENT IN MARYLAND

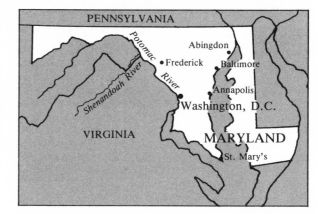

1785 _Saturday, November 5._ I crossed the Chesapeake, and found some difficulty in getting my wagon over: I missed my appointment at the college, and came late to Mr. Gough's.

STATEHOUSE AT ANNAPOLIS

Sunday, 6. Came away early, and arriving in Baltimore, preached at noon, on Heb. xi, 2-8; and at night, on Caleb's fully following the Lord. I found the means of conveyance by my carriage, or Jersey wagon, would not do.

Tuesday, 8. I preached at Annapolis to a multitude of people, part of whom were serious.

1786 _Tuesday, June 13._ Praise the Lord! There is a little religion on the Maryland side of the Potomac, and this is some comfort, without which this Allegheny would make me gloomy indeed. Sick or lame, I must try for Redstone tomorrow.

HOLDEN'S MEETINGHOUSE, QUEEN ANNE
COUNTY, MD. BUILT AROUND 1775.

Friday, December 15. We had a heavy ride to Queen Anne's chapel. I did not arrive there until near two o'clock. My soul melted for backsliders. I was much led out on Hos. xiv, 14; and hope it will never be forgotten.

THE OLD JOHN EVANS HOUSE,
SITE OF EARLY METHODIST SERMONS
IN MARYLAND

1787 *Saturday, December 15.* I had a cold ride to Annapolis; and but few to hear me on Sunday morning.

Thursday, 20. We must now direct our course for Lancaster, Virginia, through a barren route of sixty miles. This is the only uncultivated part of Maryland; and God will surely visit these people, and bless them in his own time, if they hear his voice.

1790 *Saturday, November 6.* Rode twenty-five miles to Broad Creek quarterly meeting, and preached; . . . it was a searching time. We came off, and found the wind blowing fiercely; but when we had entered the boat, we had a sudden calm: if this were not an answer to prayer, it was as I prayed. I reproved myself for a sudden and violent laugh at the relation of a man's having given an old Negro woman her liberty because she had too much religion for him.

STONE CHAPEL, NEAR WINDSOR, MD.
BUILT 1800.

1794 *Tuesday, June 17.* I rode twenty-three miles to the Stone Chapel, where I preached on Peter's denial of his Lord.

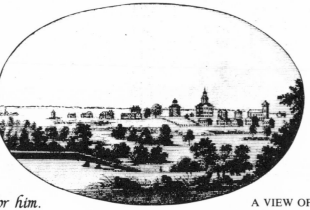

A VIEW OF ANNAPOLIS, 1797

JONES' FALLS NEAR BALTIMORE

LIGHT STREET PARSONAGE AND
CONFERENCE ROOM, BALTIMORE

1797 *Sunday, October 29. I
opened the new church in
Light Street with reading 2 Chron. vii,
12; Psalm cxxxii; Haggai ii, Mark xi.
The elders read and prayed. My subject
was Eph. ii, 19–22.*

1798 *Friday, October 5. Next
day we reached Thomson's
mill, upon Great Elk: within a mile of
this place, while going over a desperate*

*piece of road my carriage turned bottom
upwards; I was under, and thrown
down a descent of five or six feet: I
thought at first I was unhurt, but upon
examination I found my ankle was
skinned and a rib bone bruised. O, the
heat, the fall, the toil, the hunger of the
day!*

1800 *Wednesday, August 27.
I preached at the Forks
meetinghouse (fifteen miles on a carriage road), warm as it was. . . . That
evening we came with equal difficulties
to Perry Hall; but the greatest trouble
of all was that the elders of the house
were not at home: the walls, the rooms
no longer vocal, all to me appeared hung
in sackcloth. I see not the pleasant
countenances, nor hear the cheerful
voices of Mr. and Mrs. Gough! She is
in ill health, and writes: "I have left
home, perhaps never to return." This
intelligence made me melancholy.*

1805 *April 8. On Monday we
reached Fredericktown; on
Tuesday, Joshua Jones's, Sam's Creek;
and on Wednesday, 10, came into
Baltimore. . . . I have made, I
calculate, three thousand eight hundred*

*and fifty miles from the first of June,
1804, to the 10th of April, 1805.*

1810 *Sunday, March 18. Rode
ten miles to the new chapel
in Middle River Neck. I would not ride
in the coach. Will my character never be
understood? But gossips will talk. If we
want plenty of good eating and new
suits of clothes, let us come to Baltimore;
but we want souls.*

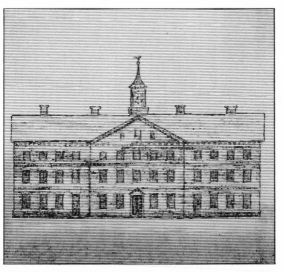

COKESBURY COLLEGE—THE FIRST METHODIST
COLLEGE IN AMERICA, NEAR ABINGDON, MD.

COKESBURY COLLEGE

A PLAN FOR ERECTING A COLLEGE, INTENDED TO ADVANCE RELIGION IN AMERICA, TO BE PRESENTED TO THE PRINCIPAL MEMBERS AND FRIENDS OF THE METHODIST EPISCOPAL CHURCH:

The College is to be built at Abingdon, in Maryland, on a healthy spot, enjoying a fine air and very extensive prospect. It is to receive for education and board the sons of the elders and preachers of the Methodist Church, poor orphans, and the sons of the subscribers and of other friends. It will be expected that all our friends who send their children to the college, will, if they be able, to pay a moderate sum for their education, and board; the rest will be taught and boarded, and, if our finances will allow it, clothed, gratis. The institution is also intended for the benefit of our young men who are called to preach, that they may receive a measure of that improvement which is highly expedient as a preparative for public service. . . .

But the expense of such an undertaking will be very large, and the best means we could think of at our late Conference to accomplish our design was, to desire the assistance of all those in every place who wish well to the work of God; who long to see sinners converted to God, and the Kingdom of Christ set up in all the earth.

All who are thus minded, and more especially our own friends who form our congregations, have an opportunity now of showing their love to the Gospel. . . . Do what you can to comfort the parents who give up their all for you, and to give their children cause to bless you. . . . And you know in doing this you lend unto the Lord; in due time He shall repay you.

Thomas Coke and Francis Asbury

HISTORICAL PERSPECTIVES ON MARYLAND AND WASHINGTON, D.C.

1634 — Charles I awards the Lord Baltimore family a tract of land in the New World.

1649 — The Maryland Assembly passes the Act of Toleration to protect Catholics from religious persecution.

1700 — Smallpox kills half the children born in the colonies.

1784 — The Methodist Episcopal Church is organized at the Christmas Conference in Baltimore.

1795 — Cokesbury College, the first Methodist experiment in higher education, burns to the ground.

1800 — Washington, D.C., becomes the national capital.

1810 — Maryland excludes free blacks from voting.

1814 — British forces capture and burn Washington, D.C., but fail to take Baltimore.
Francis Scott Key writes "The Star-Spangled Banner."

1816 — The corpse of bishop Asbury is placed in a vault under the pulpit of Eutaw Street Church, Baltimore.

THE FEDERAL CITY

1801 *Monday, April 27. We had some difficulty the next day at the ferry, being obliged to wait an hour, which made us too late for meeting in Georgetown.*

I visited Captain Lloyd Beal. I also visited Ezekiel King, son of my most dear friend, father King, in Stroud. Can a son of so many prayers be lost? Heavy strokes of Providence have afflicted his mind: he hears—he weeps—O that I may yet see him converted!

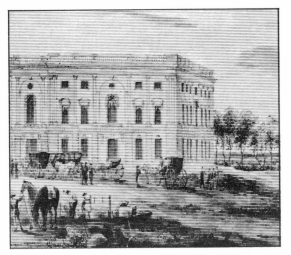

THE UNFINISHED CAPITOL, 1800

THE CITY OF WASHINGTON, 1801

1802 *March 26. On Friday it snowed most of the day; nevertheless, I rode on seven miles to Henry Foxall's, in Georgetown, where I found a shelter from the storm. I have had sore temptations, succeeded by great consolations. The want of good sleep has been a cause of suffering.*

1806 *March 3. On Monday we rode to Georgetown (D.C.).*

Tuesday, 4. I preached; my subject was, "Godliness is profitable unto all things": it was a feeling, quickening time to myself and others.

Wednesday, 5. I was employed in writing to the missionaries in the Mississippi Territory. Company does not amuse, congress does not interest me: I am a man of another world in mind and calling: I am Christ's; and for the service of his church.

1807 Wednesday, February 25. We crossed over into Maryland at Georgetown (D.C.). Surely the roads are bad! My mind is in great peace. I had to preach a kind of funeral discourse, on the death of Bishop Whatcoat, on Thursday: and on Friday I came away to Bladensburg.

1808 Wednesday, March 2. Our conference began. We laboured diligently, and in great peace. On the Sabbath I preached, and ordained deacons: souls have been converted since we are here.

Wednesday, 9. Our conference ended; and I came away to Annapolis.

1811 March 1. Friday, at Georgetown.

Sabbath, March 3. I preached for half an hour, and was fervent. At the sacrament took occasion to exhort the society. At three o'clock visited the new house in the city: I preached, though very unwell. I feel great consolation, and perfect love.

1813 March 6. Saturday, came to Georgetown, dining with Jacob Hoffman, in Alexandria.

Sabbath, 7. I changed my subject after getting into the church; and I spoke long

THE OLD TOBACCO HOUSE, WASHINGTON, D.C., WHERE METHODIST SERVICES WERE HELD, 1807-1811

EBENEZER METHODIST CHURCH, WASHINGTON, D.C. ERECTED IN 1811.

and plainly. We have news from the English Conference. It has given me an invitation to my native land, engaging to pay the expenses of the visit.

1814 *Monday, March 7. A journey of suffering by bad roads, and exposure to excessive cold, brought us to Georgetown, Maryland.*

Sunday, 13. I preached in our church in Georgetown, and met the society. We do not labour in vain. My mind is deeply impressed with the worth of souls and value of time.

WASHINGTON IN 1800

''I behold the ruins of the capitol and the President's house; the navy yard we burned ourselves. O war! War!

Journals, March 12, 1815

VIRGINIA

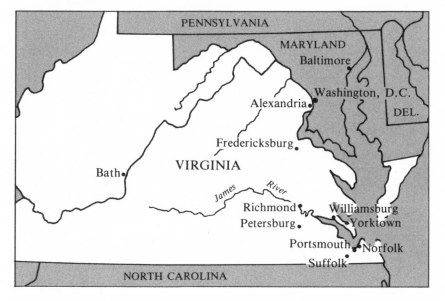

ALEXANDRIA

In 1584 Sir Walter Raleigh acting with Queen Elizabeth's blessing, sent a band of Englishmen to explore the North American coast in search of a suitable site for a colony. Raleigh's crew christened the land the explored "Virginia" in honor of their virgin queen, and returned to England for supplies to erect a colony.

The Virginia wilderness, however, was not easily tamed. Over two decades passed before a stockholding company, the London Company of Virginia, succeeded in establishing Jamestown, the first permanent English settlement in America.

For the stockholders of the company, Jamestown was at best a successful failure. In 1612 the settlers discovered that tobacco grew well in the tidewaters of Virginia. Stockholders in the colony rejoiced in the news, hoping that tobacco (a crop marketable not only as a smoking weed but also, ironically, as a medicinal cure for lung disease) would become the economic salvation of the colony. In time tobacco did bolster the region's economy, but its profitability came too late to save the debt-ridden Virginia Company. In 1624, the company declared bankruptcy, and Jamestown, originally a company colony, became the personal possession of the English king.

Virginia, the first colony, was also the largest of the English colonial possessions. A colony of great wealth, Virginia played a leading role in the political life of revolutionary America. And throughout the early national era, Virginia was known as the state of presidents as Virginians won the presidency in eight of the first nine presidential elections.

1786 *Monday, April 17. I directed my course northward, and on Thursday the twentieth reached Alexandria.*

Sunday, 23. Hail, glorious Lord! After deep exercises of body and mind, I feel a solemn sense of God in my heart. I preached by day in the courthouse, on 1 Pet. iii, 10; and in the evening at the Presbyterian church, on Luke xix, 41, 42. Alexandria must grow: and if religion prospers among them, it will be blessed. I drew a plan, and set on foot a subscription for a meetinghouse.

CHRIST CHURCH, ALEXANDRIA, VA.

MT. VERNON

THE ADDRESS OF THE BISHOPS OF THE METHODIST EPISCOPAL CHURCH

May 29, 1789

To the President of the United States

Sir:

We the bishops of the Methodist Episcopal Church, humbly beg leave, in the name of our society collectively in these United States, to express to you the warm feelings of our hearts, and our sincere congratulations, on your appointment to the presidentship of these states. We are conscious from the signal proofs you have already given, that you are a friend of mankind; and under this established idea, place as full a confidence to your wisdom and integrity, for the preservation of those civil and religious liberties which have been transmitted to us by the providence of GOD, and the glorious revolution, as we believe, ought to be reposed in man.

We have received the most grateful satisfaction, from the humble and entire dependence on the Great Governor of the universe which you have repeatedly expressed, acknowledging him the source of every blessing, and particularly of the most excellent constitution of these states, which is at present the admiration of the world, and may in future become its great exemplar for imitation: and hence we enjoy a holy expectation that you will always prove a faithful and impartial patron of genuine, vital religion—the grand end of our creation and present probationary existence. . . .

Signed in behalf of the Methodist Episcopal Church,
Thomas Coke,
Francis Asbury

GEORGE WASHINGTON

"We waited on General Washington, who received us very politely, and gave us his opinion against slavery."
Journals, May 26, 1785

VIEW OF MT. VERNON—THE SEAT OF GEORGE WASHINGTON

WILLIAMSBURG NORFOLK PORTSMOUTH

ALEXANDER MATHER

Norfolk, Portsmouth, and the country round about.

1797 *Friday, November 24. I visited my old friends, and wrote to Alexander Mather. My route, which I only guessed at, is now fixed by Norfolk, Portsmouth, Newbern, Kingston, Georgetown, and Charleston, between five and six hundred miles in little more than a month; sick or well, living or dead, my appointments go on.*

1800 *Thursday, March 13. We crossed Roanoke at Taylor's Ferry; the river was very full. Hail, ancient Virginia, once more!*

Saturday, 15, was a stormy day. One of my friends wanted to borrow or beg £50 of me: he might as well have asked me

ST. PAUL'S CHURCH, NORFOLK, VA.

for Peru. I showed him all the money I had in the world—about twelve dollars, and gave him five: strange that neither my friends nor my enemies will believe that I neither have, nor seek bags of money: well, they shall believe by demonstration, what I have ever been striving to prove—that I will live and die a poor man.

1787 *Wednesday, January 24. According to appointment, I attended at Williamsburg. I had about five from the country, and about fifteen hearers from the town, besides a few blacks and children. I spoke with freedom on, "They made light of it." I returned through the rain, but hope to receive no harm.*

1791 *Wednesday, January 5. We had a blessed time at Norfolk, whilst I applied Zech. xii, 10. Many praised the Lord aloud. I was closely employed until the moment I left town. I find the Lord has wrought in*

WILLIAM AND MARY COLLEGE, WILLIAMSBURG, VA.

SUFFOLK   PETERSBURG

1802 *Monday, March 1. We began and held close conference four days. . . . I was well pleased with the stations, as far as they went; but Portsmouth, Bertie, Roanoke, Haw River, Guilford, and Salisbury should each have had an additional preacher, if we had them; yea, Petersburg, Hanover, Williamsburg, and Richmond also; but the Lord hath not sent them and how can we make them?*

1803 *March 19. On Saturday Nicholas Snethen preached in Petersburg on 1 John ii, 15-17. On the Sabbath my subject was 2 Cor. xiii, 2. We feel the effects of intense labour in the lowlands; our habits were very feverish, and I suffer from a deep cold and oppression on my breast. We contemplate placing a proper stationed preacher in Petersburg; and the building a new brick church sixty or seventy by forty feet, and two stories high: but this, like many other of our great and good designs, may fall through.*

HOUSE AT PETERSBURG, VA.—SITE OF
FIRST METHODIST CONFERENCE IN VIRGINIA

THE JAMES RIVER ABOVE RICHMOND

Monday, March 21. I feel my infirmities, and the labour of my journeys; but my soul is cast upon the Lord in unceasing prayer that God may guide the church, and give the spirit of wisdom, and love and zeal to our conferences: we only, as we think, want more useful labourers in the vineyard, and thousands will be brought home to God in the cities, circuits, and towns this year.

1804 Monday, March 19. I preached at James Wilson's; Tuesday at Cutherell's; Wednesday at Portsmouth; Thursday at Norfolk; and on Friday and Saturday I was housed. At a meeting of the women, we laid the foundation of a female charitable society of Norfolk: similar in plan to those of New York and Baltimore, but more liberal: may this live, grow, and flourish when I am cold and forgotten!

Sabbath Day, 25. I preached at Norfolk, upon Matthew xxviii, 19–20; and at Portsmouth, in the afternoon, my subject was I Peter ii, 9–12.

Monday, 26. I preached at a new meetinghouse fourteen miles up the road towards Suffolk: here, after thirty years labour, first and last, we have a chapel; I named it Ebenezer. At Suffolk, on Tuesday, unwell as I was, labour went hard with me: I had an almost total obstruction of perspiration; but a pulpit sweat relieved me in a good degree. My soul is calm.

Wednesday, April 4. I preached . . . at Mabry's chapel, made anew; now sixty by twenty-five feet. I was a preacher here before the first house was built, thirty years ago: first an addition was made, now it is rebuilt in another form, and a gallery added for the blacks.

SLAVES ARE SHOWN HOUSING, AIRING AND VENDING TOBACCO

1806 Friday, February 14. Virginia Conference began in Norfolk; progressed peaceably, and ended on Thursday. One member opposed all petitions from the people for conference sittings: he also condemned all epistles from the sister conferences, as being too long and pompous, and as likely to make innovations. He dictated an epistle himself by way of sample, to show how epistles ought to be written: the committee of addresses wrote one too; but it was rejected, as being too much like that of the objecting member, whose epistle was rejected as being too much like himself: the conference voted that none should be sent. Strange, that such an affair should occupy the time of so many good men! Religion will do great things; but it does not make Solomons.

Wednesday, February 11. My old Virginia friends have disappeared from the earth; but it is no small consolation that they have left me their offspring— these are the children of faith and prayer. Witness the Georges, the Booths, and many others. And God has heard the prayers of the poor Negroes for their masters: surely He is no respecter of persons.

LORD CORNWALLIS SURRENDERS AT YORKTOWN, OCT. 19, 1781

1812 *Monday, March 2. I passed a night of great suffering. We came off this morning to James City, and preached in the chapel to many people— we had an evening meeting. Lodged at John Taylor's. Tuesday, we came to Williamsburg, where I preached with a full mind, but failing voice.*

On Friday I had an opportunity of giving the two families of Lucas and Stubblefield a solemn warning and charge. We crossed the river at Yorktown, now like many other towns, declining in numbers and in wickedness, because of the decrease of trade and strong drink.

HISTORICAL PERSPECTIVES ON VIRGINIA

1584 — Sir Walter Raleigh establishes the ill-fated colony of Roanoke.

1607 — England settlers erect the first permanent settlement in America at Jamestown.

1619 — The first blacks arrive in North America.

1676 — Nathaniel Bacon leads the first uprising against Royal authority as he marches on the capitol of colonial Virginia.

1776 — Richard H. Lee of Virginia introduces the resolution that the "colonies are and have right to be free and independent states."

1796 — George Washington in his "Farewell Address" urges Americans to avoid permanent military alliances and partisan politics.

1800 — General Gabriel leads slave rebellion in Richmond, Virgina.

1807 — President Jefferson places an embargo on goods to England after a British frigate fires upon the *U.S. Chesapeake* off the coast of Virginia.

1812 — Congress declares war on England.

1814 — Edward Cole asks Jefferson to lead a national abolition effort.

RICHMOND—VIRGINIA STATE CAPITAL

1798 *Friday, October 19.* We came through the dust, thirty-five miles, to Richmond: here I heard of the death of John Norman Jones, who departed in joy and peace in Charleston.

Saturday, 20. I rested in Richmond. I here must record my thanks to my ancient and firm friend, Philip Rogers, for the loan of a horse, when mine was fully worn down, and unable to stand my long and rapid rides.

1802 *March 20.* On Saturday we arrived at Richmond, and next day Nicholas Snethen preached upon the epistle to the church of Ephesus. I spoke in the afternoon upon Philip. ii, 12, 13. I had a great crowd of the most impolite, spiritually impolite hearers I have seen for many months: so much for the capital of Virginia.

1806 *Monday, February 24.* We came to Bernard Major's, Surry county: on *Tuesday* to Petersburg; and *Wednesday* to Richmond: I had no time to preach, but Joseph Crawford gave them a sermon in each place. On *Thursday* we left the capital, and came on to Lyon's, Caroline; on *Friday*, got to Fredericksburg.

1813 *February 26.* A heavy ride on *Friday* brought us to Mr. Bleaky's happy family and pleasant mansion. I have looked into

THE STATEHOUSE, RICHMOND, VA.

THE VIRGINIA STATE CAPITAL, ca. 1800

Whitehead's *Life of Wesley*—he is vilified: O, shame!

Sabbath, 28. I preached in Richmond old chapel, gave counsel to the tarrying society, baptized two infants, and ordained John Sullivan and William Whitehead deacons. I spoke again in the afternoon to a congregation made up of the young and aged. The Presbyterians and Episcopalians are striving to have places of worship.

NICHOLAS SNETHEN—ASBURY'S TRAVELING COMPANION, 1800-1804

TRAGIC THEATER FIRE OF DEC. 26, 1811, RICHMOND, VA.

1814 March 5. We reached Richmond on Saturday. Our journey hither has been through snows and excessive cold; I felt it deeply. We were careful to pray with the families where we stopped, exhorting all professors to holiness.

Sunday, 6. I preached in the old chapel; our labour shall not all be in vain. Doctor Jennings has removed to Richmond; to be useful, we hope, to the society and to himself.

NATURAL BRIDGE, VIRGINIA

In old Virginia I have administered the Word thirty years. There is a great mortality amongst the aged: our old members drop off surprisingly; but they all, by account die in the Lord, and in general, triumphantly. Now I have finished my awful tour of duty for the past month. To ride twenty and thirty miles a day; to preach, baptize, and administer the Lord's Supper; to write and answer letters, and plan for myself and four hundred preachers—O Lord, I have not desired this awful day, thou knowest! I refused to travel as long as I could, and I lived long before I took upon me the superintendency of the Methodist Church in America, and now I bear it as a heavy load; I hardly bear it, and yet dare not cast it down, for fear God and my brethren should cast me down for such an abandonment of duty. True it is, my wages are great—precious souls here, and glory hereafter.

Journals, April 8, 1804

THE CAROLINAS and GEORGIA

Far from the "Bible-belt" of today, the Deep South in colonial times was unfriendly territory for harbingers of evangelical Christianity. Infested with the plague of slavery, the southern colonies generally bowed to the interests of the wealthy plantation owners—a small yet powerful group of elites who viewed Christian missionaries as intruders bent on disrupting the social order. And in elegant Charleston, a bustling city surpassed in population only by New York, Philadelphia, and Boston, spirits flowed far more abundantly from whiskey bottles than from the hearts of jubilant Christian worshipers. At least for disciplinarians like Asbury, the southern way of life ran counter to much of the gospel they proclaimed.

But Methodism and evangelical Christianity did penetrate the southern borders. The transition from religious badland to Bible-belt occurred largely during the years of the "Second Great Awakening." This great revival of the early nineteenth century blazed across the southern prairies, singeing the souls of the free and enslaved alike. The spiritual harvest reaped by Methodist circuit riders and Baptist farmer-preachers altered the religious landscape of the South. To this day, the South is the heartland for Methodists and Baptists, the two major participants of the awakening.

1785

Monday, April 11. Preached in the courthouse at Kingston. I was entertained very kindly by Governor Caswell.

HOUSE OF GREEN HILL, NEAR LOUISBURG, N.C.—SITE OF THE FIRST CONFERENCE AFTER ORGANIZATION OF M.E. CHURCH

Tuesday, 19. Preached at the Cypress Chapel, and had many people to hear. I met Doctor Coke at Green Hill's that evening: here we held our conference in great peace.

1790

Tuesday, January 26. Since we crossed Roanoke River, we have passed through Warren, Granville, Wake, Chatham, Orange, Randolph, and Richmond counties, in North Carolina.

After passing Hedge Cock Creek, I preached at Night's chapel on, "My grace is sufficient for thee." There was some quickening, and I was blest. It is no small exercise to ride twenty miles, or more, as we frequently do, before twelve o'clock; taking all kinds of food, and lodging, and weather too, as it comes, whether it be good or bad.

NORTH CAROLINA FOOTHILLS

SCENIC NORTH CAROLINA

Tuesday, June 1. I rode about forty-five miles to Armstrong's, and next day about four o'clock reached M'Knights on the Yadkin River, in North Carolina: here the conference had been waiting for me nearly two weeks: we rejoiced together, and my brethren received me as one brought from the jaws of death.

1793 *Wednesday, March 27. We began our journey over the great ridge of mountains: we had not gone far before we saw and felt the snow; the sharpness of the air gave me a deep cold, not unlike an influenza.*

Thursday, 28. We made an early start, and came to the Beaver Dam; three years ago we slept here in a cabin without a cover. We made a breakfast at Mr. W_____'s; and then attempted the iron or stone mountain, which is steep like the roof of a house. I found it difficult and trying to my lungs to walk up it. Descending the mountain, we had to jump down the steep stairs, from two to three and four feet. At the foot of this mountain our guide left us to a man on foot; he soon declined, and we made the best of our way to Julius Dugger's ford, on Roans Creek. We came down the river, where there are plenty of large, round, rolling stones, and the stream was rapid. My horse began to grow dull: an intermittent fever and a deep cold disordered me much. . . .
Twenty years ago a rude, open loft did not affect me—now it seldom fails to injure me.

1795 *Monday, March 30. I rode forty miles to Moore's. This country improves in cultivation, wickedness, mills, and stills;*

a prophet of strong drink would be acceptable to many of these people. I believe that the Methodist preachers keep clear, both by precept and example; would to God the members did so too! Lord, have pity on weeping, bleeding Zion!

HISTORICAL PERSPECTIVES ON THE LOWER SOUTH

1670 — The Carolinas are formally created when Charles II grants to eight of his court favorites an expansive tract of wilderness below Virginia.

1712 — South Carolina separates from North Carolina.

1732 — James Oglethorpe establishes a settlement of debtors in Georgia.

1735 — John and Charles Wesley begin a missionary tour of Georgia.

1780 — Methodist preacher Jesse Lee jailed for refusing to bear arms for the North Carolina militia. Later Lee is released upon agreement to remain with the militia as a chaplain.

1793 — Eli Whitney perfects the cotton gin.

1808 — Slave trade officially ends.

1815 — Cotton boom in the Lower South.

THE FRENCH BROAD RIVER IN WESTERN NORTH CAROLINA

SLAVE SHIP TO AMERICA

1803 February 23. On Wednesday we rode through a very warm, weather-breeding day, twenty-two miles, to Tarboro, and came in about half-past two o'clock. . . . There are in this place about thirty-three families: the people have more trade than religion, more wealth than grace. We have about thirty Africans in fellowship; but no whites.

Monday, March 7. I find the way of holiness very narrow to walk in or to preach; and although I do not consider sanctification—Christian perfection, commonplace subjects, yet I make them the burden, and labour to make them the savour of every sermon. I feel, I fear for my dear lowland brethren—so much of this world's wealth; so much fulness of bread, and idleness, and strong drink. Lord, help!

1801 Friday, February 13. At Ebenezer:—the house was unfinished and the day windy and uncomfortable. Brother Whatcoat and myself held the people nearly three hours. My text was Gal. vi, 14-16.

A Solomon Reeves let me know that he had seen the Address, signed by me; and was quite confident there were no arguments to prove that slavery was repugnant to the spirit of the Gospel: what absurdities will not men defend! If the Gospel will tolerate slavery, what will it not authorize? I am strangely mistaken if this said Mr. Reeves has more grace than is necessary, or more of Solomon than the name.

1809 Sunday, February 5. We are defrauded of great numbers by the pains that are taken to keep the blacks from us; their masters are afraid of the influence of our principles. Would not an amelioration in the condition and treatment of slaves have produced more practical good to the poor Africans, than any attempt at their emancipation? . . . Who will take the pains to lead them into the way of salvation, and watch over them that they may not stray, but the Methodists? Well, now their masters will not let them come to hear us.

THE SINS OF THE SOUTH—WHISKEY AND SLAVERY

SOUTH CAROLINA

ST. PHILIP'S CHURCH, CHARLESTON

1786 *Friday, January 13. I came to Charleston: being unwell, brother Willis supplied my place.*

Sunday 15. Our congregations are large, and our people are encouraged to undertake the building of a meetinghouse this year. Charleston has suffered much—a fire about 1700—again in November, 1740—and lastly, the damage sustained by the late war: the city is now in a flourishing condition.

1788 *Wednesday, March 5. We saw a number of good dwellings and large plantations on the road leading down Ashley River. In the evening we reached the city of Charleston, having ridden about fifty miles.*

Friday, 14. Our conference began, and we had a very free, open time. On Saturday night I preached. . . . Whilst I was speaking at night, a stone was thrown against the north side of the church; then another on the south; a third came through the pulpit window, and struck near me inside the pulpit. I however continued to speak; . . . Upon the whole, I have had more liberty to speak in Charleston this visit than I ever had before, and am of opinion that God will work here.

CHARLESTON HARBOR

A VIEW NEAR CHARLESTON, 1802

"Charleston is a growing, busy, dreadfully dissipated place. The printed list of vessels in the harbour sets forth, fifty-three ships, fifty-five brigs, twenty-five sloops, twenty-five schooners, seven scows, and two barques, besides pilot boats and coasters."

Journals, February 10, 1793

GEORGETOWN   WAPPETAW   CAMDEN

1789 *Tuesday, February 10. Came, after a ride of forty miles, to Georgetown, and lectured on Isa. xl, 1-9.*

Friday, 13. Rode forty-five miles to Wappetaw; and next day arrived in Charlestown in sweet peace of soul.

Tuesday, 24. I set out for Edisto circuit, journeying up the south side of Ashley River. Here live rich and great who have houses in the city and country, and go backward and forward in their

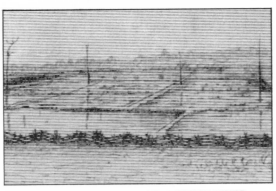

RICE FIELDS NEAR THE ASHLEY RIVER

splendid chariots; the land, however, with the exception of the rice fields, is barren, the weather is cold.

Sunday, March 1. We spent the day at Chester's [between Augusta and Edgefield]; we had very few hearers, occasioned, in part, by a black man's preaching not far distant.

1791 *Tuesday, February 8. We came a long dreary way, missed our road, and at last reached brother Session's; a distance of twenty-five miles, which our wandering made thirty miles. I rejoice to find that this desert country has gracious souls in it. O how great the change in the flight of six years! We have now many friends, and some precious souls converted to God. Glory be to the Lord most high!*

Friday, 11. We set out for Black River, from about six miles above Kingston, having Bull Run, Bramble Island, and great Pee Dee to cross. Reaching Black River, we were compelled to turn aside to Mr. S_____'s rice plantation, where we procured provender for our horses, and breakfasted on our own tea.

INDIGO FARMING ON A SOUTH CAROLINIAN PLANTATION

SPARTANBURG BEAUTY SPOT

1795 <u>Thursday</u>, <u>February 5</u>. I have been lately more subject to melancholy than for many years past; and how can I help it: the white and worldly people are intolerably ignorant of God; playing, dancing, swearing, racing; these are their common practices and pursuits. Our few male members do not attend preaching; and I fear there is hardly one who walks with God: the women and Africans attend our meetings, and some few strangers also. Perhaps it is necessary for me to know how wicked the world is, in order that I may do more as a president minister. There is some similarity between my stay here and at Bath in Virginia. O how I should prize a quiet retreat in the woods!

<u>Wednesday</u>, <u>February 11</u>, is the President's birthday; <u>Thursday</u>, <u>Friday</u>, and <u>Saturday</u>, come on the races. I intend to keep close to my room, except when attending meetings in the evenings. I am in the furnace; may I come out purified like gold! It is a dark Providence holds me here.

OLD ST. DAVID'S EPISCOPAL CHURCH, CHERAW, S.C.—SITE OF EARLY METHODIST PREACHING

<u>Thursday</u>, <u>March 26</u>. All the places I have visited this week are new, and I hope the Lord will work at some, or all of them. I exhorted our people to teach their slaves to read (this is greatly wanting); they would then understand preaching much better.

BETTING ON COCKFIGHTS—A CUSTOM RIGOROUSLY DENOUNCED BY EARLY METHODISTS

1796 <u>Monday</u>, <u>April 4</u>. Since I came into South Carolina I have ridden through Newbury, Spartanburg, Union, and Lawrence counties. There is a general complaint of the want of corn in these parts; and no wonder, when we consider the great storm which they have had, and the number of stills in the country: the people here drink their bread as well as eat it. . . . I crossed Lawson Fork at the high shoals a little below the Beauty Spot. I could not but admire the curiosity of the people—my wig was as great a subject of speculation as some wonderful animal from Africa and India would have been.

1797 _Tuesday, February 21._ A poor black, sixty years of age, who supports herself by picking oakum, and the charity of her friends, brought me a French crown and said she had been distressed on my account, and I must have her money. But no! although I have not three dollars to travel two thousand miles, I will not take money from the poor.

Saturday, March 4. At Rembert's new chapel [near Sumter] I preached on Matt. xi, 28–30, where I had some living sweetness.

Sunday, 5. Religion is reviving here among the Africans; several are joined in society: these are the poor; these are the people we are more immediately called to preach to.

1800 _Saturday, January 4._ Slow moved the Northern post on the eve of New Year's Day, and brought the heart-distressing information of the death of Washington, who departed this life December 14, 1799.

Washington, the calm, intrepid chief, the disinterested friend, first father, and temporal saviour of his country under Divine protection and direction. A universal cloud sat upon the faces of the citizens of Charleston; the pulpits clothed in black—the bells muffled—the paraded soldiery—a public oration decreed to be delivered on _Friday_, 14th of this month—a marble statue to be placed in some proper situation. . . . I am disposed to lose sight of all but Washington: matchless man! At all times he acknowledged the providence of God, and never was he ashamed of his Redeemer: we believe he died, not fearing death. In his will he ordered the manumission of his slaves—a true son of liberty in all points.

REVIVAL IN THE SLAVE QUARTERS

1801 _Saturday, January 24._ This is an unhappy country: it is thinly settled, and many are moving away to Georgia and the Natchez; our societies are small, and the prospect low. Too often, when any rise in their circumstances, they seek for offices, or become slave traders, and much too great to be Methodists.

1805 _Tuesday, December 10._ I doubt if in Charleston we have joined more than one hundred and seventy-eight members of the fair skin in twenty years; and seldom are there more than fifty or sixty annually returned: death, desertion, backsliding: poor fickle souls, unstable as water, light as air, bodies and minds!

1810 _December 20._ Thursday came to Columbia. Taylor, of the senate of the United States lent his house for the session of our conference. We have pleasing letters from York, Genesee, Jersey, Maryland, Virginia, old North and South Carolinas: rich and poor coming to God. . . . _Saturday_, our conference began in great order, peace, and love.

THE STATEHOUSE IN COLUMBIA, SOUTH CAROLINA

GEORGIA—LAND OF WESLEY & WHITEFIELD

1796 *Friday, March 11. I saw how the flood had ploughed up the streets of Augusta: I walked over the ruins for nearly two miles, viewing the deep gulfs in the main street. I suppose they would crucify me if I were to tell them it is the African flood; but if they could hear me think, they would discover this to be my sentiment. I have ridden about one hundred and ninety miles from Charleston into Georgia; I have attended four meetings; and have not had, in all, above six hundred hearers.*

1801 *Friday, November 20. We started, hungry and cold, crossing at Malone's mill, a branch of Oconee, and came to Henry Pope's in Oglethorpe. We have ridden about eighty miles this week of short and cold days. Why should a living man complain?—but to be three months together upon the frontiers, where, generally, you have but one room and fireplace, and half a dozen folks about you, strangers perhaps, and their family certainly (and they are not usually small in these plentiful new countries), making a crowd—and this is not all; for here you may meditate if you can, and here you must preach, read, write, pray, sing, talk, eat, drink, and sleep—or fly into the woods. . . . But I cheer myself as well as I may with songs in the night—with Wesley's, Watt's, and Stennett's "Sight of Canaan," in four hymns.*

JAMES OGLETHORPE—TRUSTEE OF THE COLONY OF GEORGIA

SLAVES WORKING THE COTTON GIN

"There are many hindrances to the work of God in this section of the country . . . amongst the first are Sabbath markets, rum, races, and rioting. . . ."

Journals, December 24, 1803

1788 *Tuesday, April 1. We crossed the Savannah at the Forks, and came where I much wanted to be—in Georgia. Nevertheless, I fear I shall have but little freedom here.*

1791 *Saturday, March 19. I have ridden about two hundred and fifty miles in Georgia, and find the work, in general, very dead. The peace with the Creek Indians, the settlement of new lands, good trade, buying slaves, &c., to take up the attention of the people.*

1793 *Monday, January 14. I am now bound for Savannah, where I may see the former walks of a dear Wesley and Whitefield, with whom I hope to meet in the new Jerusalem.*

WESLEY CHAPEL, SAVANNAH, GA. DEDICATED BY
BISHOP ASBURY IN 1813

WHITEFIELD'S ORPHAN HOUSE, SAVANNAH, GA.

Tuesday, 29. We reach Savannah. Next day I rode twelve miles along a fine, sandy road to view the ruins of Mr. Whitefields's Orphan House: we found the place, and having seen the copperplate, which I recognized, I felt very awful; the wings are yet standing though much injured, and the school house still more. It is reported that Mr. Whitefield observed, whilst eating his last dinner in the house, "This house was built for God; and cursed be the man that puts it to any other use."

BEYOND THE MOUNTAINS

America has long been a land of travellers, or more precisely, of westward travellers. In the early national era, tens of thousands of adventurous or disgruntled Americans packed their scant belongings into saddlebags and wagons and scaled the Appalachian highlands to find a new home on the American frontier. Though many perished along the rugged steeps, in time the courageous survivors tamed the wilderness and carved a new civilization out of the isolated terrain.

Asbury loved the spirit of the American pioneers, but he also pitied their lack of vital religion. It was the Methodist mission, he insisted, to "spread scriptural holiness across the land," and this included every nook and cranny on the frontier. Hence, without waiting for settled establishments, Asbury sent his men beyond the mountains. With the earliest emigrants, Methodist circuit preachers climbed the bluffs and forded the streams, while taking the gospel message to the furthermost ends of the states. The vigor of Methodism today within the states of Ohio, Indiana, Kentucky and Tennessee is to a large degree the consequence of the sacrificial labor of the early itinerants who risked their all for the sake of the Kingdom.

PITTSBURGH IN 1790

1784 *Thursday, July 1. We began to ascend the Allegheny, directing our course towards Redstone. We passed the Little Meadows, keeping the route of Braddock's road for about twenty-two miles, along a rough pathway: arriving at a small house, and halting for the night, we had, literally, to lie as thick as three in a bed.*

1786 *Monday, June 26. Preached in Coxe's Fort on the Ohio River, on "Trust in the Lord, and do good, so shalt thou dwell in the land." . . . We found it necessary to return, they said twelve, but I thought fifteen miles. We were lost in the woods, and it rained all the way. We, however, came in about eight o'clock, and about ten laid ourselves down to rest in peace.*

1787 *Tuesday, July 31. Rode to the Springs (Bath), much tried in spirit. I gave myself to reading and prayer.*

Tuesday and Wednesday, August 7, 8. Had very few to hear, so I gave them up: everything that is good is in low estimation at this place. I will return to my own studies: if the people are determined to go to hell, I am clear of their blood.

WEST VIRGINIA and OHIO

1788 *Thursday, July 10. We had to cross the Allegheny Mountain again, at a bad passage. Our course lay over mountains and through valleys, and the mud and mire were such as might scarcely be expected in December. We came to an old, forsaken habitation in Tyger's Valley. Here our horses grazed about, while we boiled our meat.*

Sunday, 13. O, how glad should I be of a plain, clean plank to lie on, as preferable to most of the beds; and where the beds are in a bad state, the floors are worse. The gnats are almost as troublesome here as the mosquitoes in the lowlands of the seaboard. This country will require much work to make it tolerable. The people are, many of them, of the boldest cast of

SULPHUR SPRINGS OR BATH, W. VA.—SUMMER HEALTH RESORT
OF THE LATE 18TH CENTURY

adventurers, and with some the decencies of civilized society are scarcely regarded.

1789 *Friday, August 7. Came to Bath.*

Saturday, 8. My soul has communion with God, even here. When I behold the conduct of the people who attend the Springs, particularly the gentry, I am led to thank God that I was not born to riches; I rather bless God, that I am not in hell, and that I cannot partake of pleasure with sinners.

1790 *Sunday, July 11. The morning was rainy. About noon I set out for the Sweet Springs, and preached on 1 Cor. i, 23–29. A few of the gentry were kind enough to come and hear—and some were enraptured with the sermon; for—it was very like the subject. The three following days I rested, and was very unwell. I had no place to preach, but under the trees, and preaching here seems unseasonable with the people except on Sundays.*

EMIGRANTS CROSSING THE ALLEGHENIES

REHOBOTH METHODIST CHURCH,
UNION, W. VA.

1792 Sunday, May 20. I preached at Rehoboth, on Isa. iv, 12; there was no great move: brothers Hope Hull and Philip Cox both spoke after me. ''Weary world, when will it end?''

My mind and body feel dull and heavy, but still my soul drinks deeper into God. We rode about one hundred and sixty miles from the rich Valley to Greenbrier conference; talking too much, and praying too little, caused me to feel barrenness of soul.

1795 Monday, May 18. Next morning breakfasted with John Hite, and then came to Harper's Ferry, where the impending rocks impress the mind of the traveller with terror; and should they fall would crush him to pieces: this scene is truly awful and romantic.

1796 Friday, May 20. We rode forty miles to Indian Creek, about fifteen miles above the mouth. We had no place to dine until we arrived at father Cook's, about six o'clock. If I could have regular food and sleep, I could stand the fatigue I have to go through much better; but this is impossible under some circumstances. To sleep four hours, and ride forty miles without food or fire, is hard; but we had water enough in the rivers and creeks. I shall have ridden nearly one thousand miles on the western waters before I leave them; I have been on the waters of Nolachucky to the mouth of Clinch; on the north, middle, and south branches of Holston; on New River, Green Brier, and by the head springs of Monongahela. . . . Ah! if I were young again!

1803 September 6. On Tuesday I preached . . . at John Spahr's. I came with Reason Pumphrey down the great hill, to the Ohio. Wednesday brought us to Charlestown, the capital of Brook County, situated at the mouth of Buffalo, eighty miles from Pittsburgh. We found the Ohio so low, that the boat of Colonel Lewis, who is going to explore the Mississippi, would not float over the flats.

HARPER'S FERRY—LOOKING ACROSS AND DOWN THE POTOMAC,
WITH THE SHENANDOAH COMING IN ON RIGHT MIDDLE

FLATBOAT ON THE OHIO, NEAR WHEELING, W. VA.

BRUSH CREEK CHAPEL—FIRST M.E. CHURCH
IN THE NORTHWEST TERRITORY

1803 *Saturday, September 24. I rode to Chillicothe, fifteen miles, through lands generally rich. We passed some of those mounds and intrenchments which still astonish all who visit this country, and give rise to many conjectures respecting their origin: "Shadows, clouds, and darkness rest" and will rest "upon them."*

In the statehouse, which also

FIRST METHODIST HOUSE AT CHILLICOTHE.
ERECTED 1807.

COURTHOUSE AT CHILLICOTHE—THE FIRST CAPITAL OF OHIO

answers for a courthouse, I preached to about five hundred hearers, and would have had more had not the rain prevented. Chillicothe stands upon the point of confluence of the Scioto River and Paint Creek.

Tuesday, 27. We stopped at Ohio Brush Creek, fifteen miles; dined in haste with George Spurgin, and bent our course to George Rogers's, at Darlington's ferry—this was a stretching ride.

Wednesday, 28. It is wonderful to contemplate the effects of American enterprise exhibited in the State of Ohio: it is but four years since Zane opened the road for the general government through the wilderness so lately called, and now there are the towns of Marietta at the mouth of the Muskingum of about one thousand houses; Cincinnati, containing as many; Hamilton, of five hundred houses: and many others whose names are scarcely fixed.

TRAVELS INTO OHIO

CAMPUS MARTIUS IN 1791

1807 *August 24. We crossed over into the State of Ohio on Monday: and I gave them a sermon in the courthouse at St. Clairsville.*

Friday, September 4. We came away to Chillicothe: O, the mud and the trees in the path! Reading closely on Saturday. In our neat, new house I preached on the Sabbath morning to about five hundred hearers, on 1 Peter iv, 17-18; I spoke about an hour. There are some pleasing and some unpleasing accounts here; some little trouble in the society, but great prospects all around the country.

1808 *August 17. We dined at brother Cutler's on Wednesday, and came on, through Xenia, to Frederick Bonner's, Little Miami; thirty-two miles. I have more than once put the wrong foot foremost in my journeys*

west: the spring will not do because of wet, and deep, and dismal roads: the summer's extreme heat, and the small and the green flies make disagreeable travelling. I make a decree, but not of the Medes and Persians, never, in future, to cross the mountains before the first of September, nor leave Carlisle before the first of October.

Thursday, September 1. I preached at the chapel, Little Miami. We had a full house at a short notice. I was grieved to see an unfeeling man take away a poor widow's horse for debt: but brother Gatchell soon relieved me—he paid the debt, and restored the horse to the distressed woman to be hers for life.

HISTORICAL PERSPECTIVES ON THE OLD NORTHWEST

1785 — Land Ordinance Act provides that the acreage of the Old Northwest be sold to help pay off the national debt.

1787 — Northwest Ordinance Act prohibits slaves in the Old Northwest.

1788 — The Ohio Company of Associates plants the settlement of Marietta at the junction of the Ohio and Muskingum Rivers.

1795 — General "Mad Anthony" Wayne's victory over the Indians at the Battle of Fallen Timbers opens the northwest for rapid immigration.

1803 — Ohio admitted to the Union.

1811 — Construction on the National Road connecting Cumberland, Maryland with Wheeling, [West] Virginia begins.

1861 — During the Civil War, western counties of Virginia separated from the Confederate state. Two years later, West Virginia was admitted as a state.

FIRST METHODIST CHURCH AT MILFORD, OHIO.
ERECTED 1816.

1809 *August 31. Next day (Thursday) we made eighteen miles to Springfield, where I preached by appointment; we had about four hundred people: I wanted my breakfast, I wanted strength, and I wanted sleep. Brother Boehm preached at Zanesville, named after Colonel Zane, who so kindly entertained us at Wheeling: he is an extraordinary man, and the history of his life strange.*

September 21. On Thursday we came down Little and Great Miami; the rich lands of these rivers are occupied by New Lights, Shakers, Methodists—and sinners to be sure.

Sabbath, 24. I spoke in the new chapel in Milford: brothers Lakin and Boehm also spoke. I feel the importance of the approaching conference.

1810 *September 13. Thursday, we took our departure from the banks of the beautiful river (the Ohio), beautiful indeed! How rich the hanging scenery of its wood-crowned hills! Our route was towards and near the Hocking River, a rude, toilsome way: we were glad to stop a moment, and dine at Esquire Rilshure's.*

Thursday, 27. We crossed the Little Miami; dined at Taulman's; and came into Cincinnati. . . . Friday, Henry Boehm preached in German: I added an exhortation in English.

Sunday, 30. I preached morning and evening. . . . Monday, met the society. Tuesday, we bade farewell to our attentive and affectionate friends in Cincinnati. The great river was covered with mist until nine o'clock, when the airy curtain rose slowly from the waters, gliding along in expanded and silent majesty.

"Mr. Van Meeter told me that a boy cultivated about twelve acres, which would yield him about seven hundred bushels of Indian corn: now what do these people want with slaves? They have wisely prohibited their introduction into the state."
Journals, September 21, 1803

CINCINNATI, OHIO, AT 1800

TENNESSEE and KENTUCKY

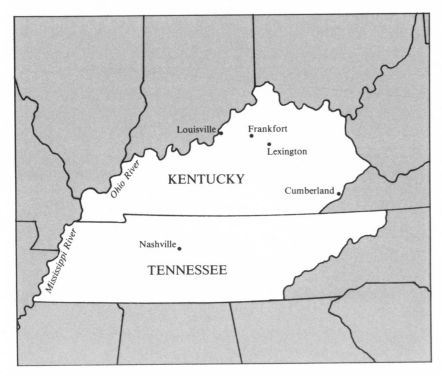

Louisville
Frankfort
Lexington
KENTUCKY
Cumberland
Ohio River
Mississippi River
Nashville
TENNESSEE

1790

Tuesday, April 6. We were compelled to ride through the rain, and crossed the Stone Mountain: those who wish to know how rough it is may tread in our path. What made it worse to me was, that while I was looking to see what was become of our guide, I was carried off with full force against a tree that hung across the road some distance from the ground, and my head received a very great jar, which however, was lessened by my having a hat that was strong in the crown. We came on to the dismal place

called Roan's Creek, which was pretty full. Here we took a good breakfast on our tea, bacon, and bread. Reaching Watauga, we had to swim our horses, and ourselves to cross in a canoe; up the Iron Mountain we ascended, where we had many a seat to rest, and many a weary step to climb.

Tuesday, 13. We came back to Amis's—a poor sinner. He was highly offended that we prayed so loud in his house. He is a distiller of whisky, and boasts of gaining £ 300 per annum by the brewing of his poison. We talked very plainly. . . . He said he did not desire me to trouble myself about his soul. Perhaps the greatest offence was given by my speaking against distilling and slave holding.

CAMPSITE FOR A PARTY OF EMIGRANTS EN ROUTE TO TENNESSEE

1793 Friday, March 29. We took our journey deliberately. We passed Doe River at the fork, and came through the Gap; a most gloomy scene—not unlike the Shades of Death in the Allegheny Mountain. . . . We prayed, and came on to a kind people; but to our sorrow we find it low times for religion on Holston and Watauga Rivers.

1796 Saturday, April 16. We set off at six o'clock, and directed our course up Toe River; thence up the Rocky Creek through the gap of the Yellow Mountain, to the head waters of Doe River; we had to ride till eight o'clock at night.

Sunday, May 1. My mind is variously exercised as to future events—whether it is my duty to continue to bear the burden I now bear, or whether I had not better retire to some other land. I am not without fears, that a door will be opened to honour, ease, or interest; and then farewell to religion in the American Methodist Connexion; but death may soon end all these thoughts and quiet all these fears.

1797 Saturday, March 25. We were escorted by three brave young Dutchmen. After riding three miles we began to scale the rocks, hills, and mountains, worming through pathless woods, to shun a deep ford. I thought, ride I must; but no—the company concluded to walk. I gave my horse the direction of himself, under Providence. I had to step from rock to rock, hands and feet busy; but my breath was soon gone, and I gave up the cause, and took horse again, and resolved that I would ride down the hills, although I had not

ridden up them. At last (hit or miss, Providence is all) into the path we came, and thence kept down the river and over to Little Doe bearing down the stream. When we had passed through the Gap we wished to feed; but the man had no corn to sell. We tried, man and horse, to reach Nathan Davies's; where we arrived, and were made comfortable.

FLAX SCUTCHING BEE IN RURAL TENNESSEE

Sunday, 26. I am of opinion it is as hard, or harder, for the people of the west to gain religion as any other. When I consider where they came from, where they are, and how they are, and how they are called to go farther, their being unsettled, with so many objects to take their attention, with the health and good air they enjoy; and when I reflect that not one in a hundred came here to get religion, but rather to get plenty of good land, I think it will be well if some or many do not eventually lose their souls.

99

CAMPSITE REVIVAL

1775 — Opening of the trans-Appalachia area with settlements in what is now eastern Tennessee.

1782 — First regularly appointed Methodist circuit riders sent over the mountains.

1790 — First U.S. Census registers 74,000 and 36,000, respectively, in the Kentucky and Tennessee territories.

1792 — Kentucky admitted to the Union.

1796 — Tennessee admitted to the Union.

1801 — Cane Ridge Camp Meeting attracts an estimated crowd of 25,000 worshippers and is declared by many observers "the greatest outpouring of the Spirit since Pentecost."

1800

Sunday, October 19. I rode to Nashville, long heard of, but never seen by me until now; some thought the congregation would be small, but I believed it would be large; not less than one thousand people were in and out of the stone church; which, if floored, ceiled, and glazed, would be a grand house.

Monday, 20. We came by Mansker's to Drake's creek meetinghouse, at the close of a sacramental solemnity, that had been held four days by Craighead, Hodge, Rankin, M'Gee, and Mr. Adair, Presbyterian officiating

ministers; we came in, and brother M'Kendree preached . . . after him brother Whatcoat, . . . I also spoke. . . . It is supposed there are one thousand souls present, and double that number heard the Word of life on Sunday.

Tuesday, 21. Yesterday and especially during the night, were witnessed scenes of deep interest. In the intervals between preaching, the people refreshed themselves and horses and returned upon the ground. The stand was in the open air, embosomed in a wood of lofty beech trees. The ministers of God, Methodists and Presbyterians, united their labours and mingled with the childlike simplicity of primitive times. Fires blazing here and there dispelled the darkness and the shouts of the redeemed captives, and the cries of precious souls struggling into life, broke the silence of midnight. The weather was delightful; as if heaven smiled, whilst mercy flowed in abundant streams of salvation to perishing sinners. We suppose there were at least thirty souls converted at this meeting. I rejoice that God is visiting the sons of the Puritans, who are candid enough to acknowledge their obligations to the Methodists.

1802

Monday, September 13. I rode alone to Edward Coxe's, near Shote's ford, upon Holston. On Tuesday and Wednesday we rested; and on Thursday we rode to Cashe's, near Jonesboro, Tennessee.

Friday, 17. I attended a camp meeting which continued to be held four days: there may have been fifteen hundred souls present. . . . We had a shaking, and some souls felt convicting and converting grace.

THE FRONTIER CAMP MEETING

1803 *Friday, October 14. We came to Hunts's, at Claibornes courthouse (Taxewell); and next day reached Martin Stubblefield's. What a road we have passed! Certainly the worst on the whole continent, even in the best weather; yet, bad as it was, there were four or five hundred crossing the rude hills whilst we were: I was powerfully struck with the consideration, that there were at least as many emigrants annually from east to west: we must take care to send preachers after these people.*

STATEHOUSE AT NASHVILLE. ERECTED 1802

1812 *Friday, October 30. We came away late to Nashville, stopping on our way to speak to the widow Bowen, the daughter of my ancient friend, the late General Russell; this lady hath three daughters who profess religion: surely we have not prayed in vain. We found the river high on Saturday; Mr. Hobbs, the jailer, kindly took us in; but we are not prisoners, but of hope—but of the Lord.*

Sabbath, November 1. I preached in the new, neat brick house, thirty-four feet square, with galleries. Twelve years ago I preached in the old stone house, taken down since to make a site for the statehouse. The latter house exceeds the former in glory, and stands exactly where our house of worship should by right have stood; but we bear all things patiently. This is a pentecostal day to my soul. Hail, all hail, eternal glory!

THE KENTUCKY WILDERNESS

1790 *Wednesday, April 7. Now it is that we must prepare for danger, in going through the wilderness. I received a faithful letter from brother Poythress in Kentucky, encouraging me to come. This letter I think well deserving of publication. I found the poor preachers indifferently clad, with emancipated bodies, and subject to hard fare; yet I hope they are rich in faith.*

Sunday, 11. My soul is humbled before God, waiting to see the solution of this dark providence. The man of the house is gone after some horses supposed to be stolen by Indians. I have been near fainting; but my soul is revived again, and my bodily strength somewhat renewed. If these difficulties, which appear to impede my path, are designed to prevent my going to Kentucky, I hope to know shortly.

Sunday, May 9. We travelled about fifty miles; and next day forty-five miles, and reached Madison courthouse, passing the branches of Rock Castle River: on our journey we saw the rock whence the river derives its name; it is amazing and curious, with appearances the most artificial I have ever seen—it is not unlike an old church or castle in Europe.

Tuesday, 11. Crossed Kentucky River. I was strangely outdone for want of sleep, having been greatly deprived of it in my journey through the wilderness; which is like being at sea, in some respects, and in others worse. Our way is over mountains, steep hills, deep rivers, and muddy creeks; a thick growth of reeds for miles together; and no inhabitants but wild beasts and savage men. . . .

I saw the graves of the slain—

WATER TRAVEL ON THE FRONTIER

twenty-four in one camp. . . . I received an account of the death of another wicked wretch who was shot through the heart, although he vaunted, with horrid oaths, that no Creek Indian could kill him. These are some of the melancholy accidents to which the country is subject for the present; as to the land, it is the richest body of fertile soil I have ever beheld.

Thursday, 13. Being court time, I preached in a dwelling house at Lexington and not without some feeling. The Methodists do but little here—others lead the way. . . .

Our conference was held at brother Masterson's, a very comfortable house, and kind people. We went through our business in great love and harmony. . . . My soul has been blessed among these people, and I am exceedingly pleased with them. I would not, for the worth of all the place, have been prevented in this visit, having no doubt but that it will be for the good of the present rising generation. It is true, such exertions of mind and body are trying; but I am supported under it: if souls are saved, it is enough.

1792 *Monday, April 2.* We entered the wilderness and reached Robinson's station. Two of the company were on foot, carrying their packs; and women there are with their children. These encumbrances make us move slowly and heavily.

Tuesday, 3. We reached Richland Creek, and were preserved from harm. About two o'clock it began to rain, and continued most of the day. After

crossing the Laurel River, which we were compelled to swim, we came to Rock Castle station, where we found such a set of sinners as made it next to hell itself. Our corn here cost us a dollar per bushel.

FIRST METHODIST CHURCH IN KENTUCKY
AT MASTERSON STATION, NEAR LEXINGTON

1800 *Tuesday, October 14.* We began our march for Cumberland. We were told by two persons that we could not cross the Rolling Fork of Salt River; I judged we could, and as I thought, so it was—we forded it with ease. We came up a solitary path east of the level woods, and struck into the road to Lee's ferry. For ten miles of the latter part of this day's

journey, we rode through barrens of hickory, shrub oak, and hazelnut; thirty miles, if not thirty-five is the amount of this day's work; in the morning there was a very great damp, and in the afternoon it was, I thought, as warm as the west of Georgia.

1803 *October 10.* On Monday we took the path for Madison, crossing the Kentucky River at Combe's ferry: we put in at Christopher Irwine's. On Tuesday we stopped at Wood's—in the woods: his house being unfinished, there were masons, and carpenters, and gentlemen, and riflemen, and whisky topers, besides the gnats and bats, which ever and anon, flew in and out: we quitted our purgatory upon paying two and a half dollars for three of us.

1805 *Wednesday, October 16.* We meet crowds of people directing their march to the fertile West: their sufferings for the present are great; but they are going to present abundance, and future wealth for their children: in ten years, I think, the new State will be one of the most flourishing in the Union.

THE CUMBERLAND GAP

STATEHOUSE, FRANKFORT, KY.

THE FALLS OF THE OHIO RIVER AT LOUISVILLE, KY.

1810 *October 6. Saturday we started away for Lexington, and were well soaked with a glorious shower when about nine miles from the town. Henry Boehm preached.*

Wednesday, 17. Came by lowly seated Frankfort. Here are elegant accommodations provided for those who make the laws, and those who break them; but there is no house of God.

THE VILLAGE OF FRANKFORT, KY., ca. 1815

1812 *October 12. We came over to Kentucky on Monday and reached noisy Lexington: there was company enough, and little quiet through the night.*

On Friday I preached in the representative chamber in Frankfort. I conversed with some of the respectables and found one who had made one of my company twenty-three years ago in a journey through the wilderness.

Tuesday, 20. We came down to Baregrass Creek. What is called the Baregrass Settlement is the garden of the State. It is a low, level country, and in wet seasons must be sickly as it is now.

Wednesday, 21. I preached in Louisville at eleven o'clock in our neat brick house, thirty-four by thirty-eight feet. I had a sickly, serious congregation. This is a growing town, and a handsome place, but the falls or ponds make it unhealthy: we lodged at Farquer's.

THE FRONTIER TERRITORIES

FORDING THE WABASH

Asbury had a special love for the American frontier. Early in his career he sensed the potential for the spread of evangelical Christianity on the back country, and his zeal for reaching the western pioneers with the gospel grew stronger with time. The following lines from a letter he wrote late in life to Zachary Myles portray Asbury's never ending resolve for winning the West for Christ.

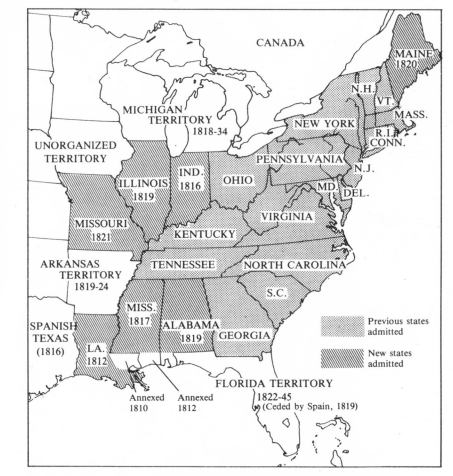

Buncombe, North Carolina
December 3, 1812

My dear Brother:

... With humble surprise, I found that our western conferences gave an account of about 12,000 increase. Emigrations, earthquakes, &c. have been made favourable to the work of God. We have high expectations, that the light affliction will work for our good; ... and that thousands, if not millions, shall see the salvation of the Gospel.

We shall find it necessary to appoint another conference in the West, upon Mississippi, and form an annual episcopal circuit of ten conferences.

Francis Asbury

1808 *Wednesday, September 1. After crossing White River, we came to Lawrenceburg, the first town in the Indian territory. In this wild there may be twenty thousand souls already. I feel for them.*

WRIGHT'S HOUSE NEAR EDWARDSVILLE—SITE OF THE FIRST
METHODIST CONFERENCE IN ILLINOIS, 1817

ILLINOIS   MISSOURI

1803 *Saturday, October 8. I felt my mind devoutly fixed on God. I accomplished two things in conference: viz. 1. Forming the Ohio circuits into a district; 2. Sending two missionaries to Natchez, and one to the Illinois.*

1809 *Saturday, October 14. We have in Mississippi, fifteen traveling and eight local preachers; and three hundred and sixty members: if spared and so directed, I shall see that country and Canada before I die.*

BETHEL MEETINGHOUSE NEAR
EDWARDSVILLE. THE FIRST METHODIST
CHURCH IN ILLINOIS. BUILT IN 1805.

Francis Asbury to Henry Smith
August 11, 1810

"Brother McKendree is gone to Missouri, if he does not faint or die by the way. He is in ill health. Pray for him, for me, for all."

MISSISSIPPI AND BEYOND

A HILLSIDE VIEW OF NATCHEZ, ca. 1820

1810 *Sunday, October 28. We have an open door set wide to us in Mississippi; the preachers there sent but one messenger to conference—they could not spare more; they keep their ground like soldiers of Christ, and men of God who care for the cause and work of the Lord.*

1811 *Saturday, October 26. Wrote a serious letter to Samuel Dunwoody, on his taking charge of the Mississippi district. What a field is opened, and opening daily in this New World!*

1812 *November 3. Tuesday, busy in writing: I conclude that next year we shall visit and hold a conference in Mississippi, if so directed and permitted.*

Saturday, 21. If we meet the Mississippi Conference, as appointed, in November, 1813, we shall have gone entirely round the United States in forty-two years: but there will be other States: well, God will raise up men to make and to meet conferences in them also, if we remain faithful as a people.

1814 *Sabbath, October 2. Poor bishops—sick, lame, and in poverty! I had wished to visit Mississippi, but the injury received by Bishop M'Kendree being so great that it is yet doubtful whether he will so far recover as to be present at the South Carolina Conference. I must decline going: I live in God.*

1815 *Wednesday, October 4. I have visited the South thirty times in thirty-one years. I wish to visit Mississippi, but am resigned.*

ADDITIONS TO THE UNION	DATE OF STATEHOOD
Vermont	March 4, 1791
Kentucky	June 1, 1792
Tennessee	June 1, 1796
Ohio	March 1, 1803
Louisiana	April 30, 1812
Indiana	December 11, 1816
Mississippi	December 10, 1817
Illinois	December 3, 1818
Alabama	December 14, 1819
Maine	March 15, 1820
Missouri	August 10, 1821

YEARS OF DECLINE—1811-1815

Though Asbury shared little in common with the eminent Ben Franklin, he would have agreed with Franklin's witty comment: "How many observe Christ's birthday. How few his precepts. O! 'tis easier to keep holidays than commandments."

The truism which humored Franklin, haunted Asbury. For five decades Asbury labored to narrow the gap between professors and practitioners of the faith. Defining Methodism as disciplined Christianity, Asbury insisted that Methodists must be converted or at least awakened sinners who aspired for holy living.

By 1811 Asbury had encircled the continent some three dozen times. If aging and deteriorating health slowed his pace, it never altered his message nor tarnished his zeal. To the end Asbury voiced disdain over slavery, his high expectations for winning the West, and his ambition for Christian perfection this side of the grave.

1811 *Friday, August 9. My flesh is ready to think it something for a man of sixty-six, with a highly inflamed and painful foot, to ride nearly four hundred miles on a stumbling, starting horse, slipping or blundering over desperate roads from Paris to this place in twelve days.*

Sabbath, 11. I preached in Boehm's Chapel [Lancaster, County, Pa.]. There is a camp meeting thirty miles distant from hence; but I cannot be there—I have the will, but I want time and strength.

Monday, November 18, the day of my arrival, my knee was stricken with acute rheumatic pain; I applied a strongly-drawing blister, and remained still and quiet. Yesterday, I tried a poultice, and I now begin to walk with some ease.

Tuesday, 19. Hillard Judge is chosen chaplain to the legislature of South Carolina; and O, great Snethen is chaplain to Congress! So; we begin to partake of the honour that cometh from man: now is our time of danger. O Lord, keep us pure, keep us correct, keep us holy!

Monday, 25. We had a serious shock of an earthquake this morning—a sad presage of future sorrows, perhaps. Lord, make us ready!

Friday, 29, at Camden [S.C.], to preside in conference.

THE GREAT EARTHQUAKE AT NEW MADRID

Friday, December 6. Our conference rose this day. Scarcely have I seen such harmony and love. There are eighty-five preachers stationed. The increase, within its bounds, is three thousand three hundred and eighty. We had a great deal of faithful preaching, and there were many ordinations. I received letters from the extremities, and the center of our vast continent, all pleasing, all encouraging.

AN INDIGO PLANTATION NEAR CHARLESTON, S.C.

A ROADSIDE SCENE NEAR CHARLESTON

1812

Wednesday, January 1. A steady ride of thirty-eight miles brought us into Charleston. The highways were little occupied by travellers of any kind, which was the more providential to me, for my lameness and my light fly cart would have made a shock of the slightest kind disagreeable. I was anxious also to pass this first day of the new year in undisturbed prayer.

Tuesday, February 4. We have made seven hundred miles since we left Camden, through frost, floods, cold, and hunger; poor men, and poor horses! Well, this life is not eternal.

Thursday, 20. A charge had been brought against me for ordaining a slave; but there was no further pursuit of the case when it was discovered that I was ready with my certificates to prove his freedom; the subject of contention was nearly white, and his respectable father would neither own nor manumit him.

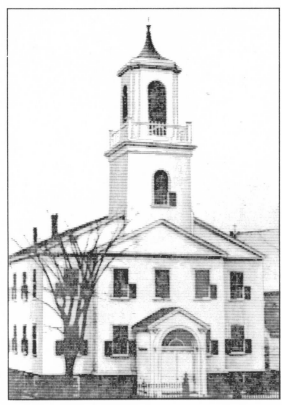

THE FIRST M.E. CHURCH IN LYNN, MASS. ERECTED 1791.

Thursday, June 18, we dined at Stone's tavern in Framingham [Mass.]; they had nearly been as wild as Indians when we prayed. I have felt sick enough to be in bed. We came to Lynn.

Sabbath, 21. I preached. The chapel, saving the pews and the steeple, is beautiful. We had an ordination. The

proclamation of the President of the United States is out, to inform us that there is a war between our people and the English people: my trust is in the living God.

Wednesday, August 5. We came along down the turnpike, and rough we found it. Farewell to Merwine's—I lodge no more there; whisky—hell; as most of the taverns here are. Our Thursday's ride brought us rapidly to Lehigh; we crossed at the ford, and had little time to admire the beautiful country above and below. The Germans are decent in their behavior in this neighborhood; and would be more so, were it not for vile whisky: this is the prime curse of the United States, and will be, I fear much, the

HENRY BOEHM

ruin of all that is excellent in morals and government in them. Lord, interpose thine arm! Lord, send thy gospel to these Germans! We lodge with George Custos, Wyomissing [Pa.].

A VIEW OF READING, PENNSYLVANIA

Friday, 7. I am still; I abstain. In the evening we had an assemblage of people, and brother Boehm spoke to them in German.

Friday, December 25. Christmas Day was a day of fasting, and we dined one hundred at our house on bread and water, and a little tea or coffee in the evening. Funds are low; but our Church is inured to poverty, and the preachers may be called the poor of this world, as well as their flocks.*

The Second War for Independence, 1812-1815

"I feel a deep concern for the old and the world; calamity and suffering are coming upon them both: I shall make but few remarks on this unhappy subject; it is one on which the prudent will be silent; but I must needs say it is an evil day."

<u>Journals</u>, August 8, 1812

A BATTLE AT SEA, 1812

A VIEW OF EARLY WASHINGTON FROM THE PRESIDENT'S HOUSE

1813 Thursday, February 25. We passed through Petersburg to Cox's, on the James River. Here flesh failed, and I wished for rest and found it. A heavy ride on Friday brought us to Mr. Bleaky's happy family and pleasant mansion. I have looked into Whiteheads's Life of Wesley—he is vilified: O, shame!

Saturday, March 6, came to Georgetown, dining with Jacob Hoffman, in Alexandria [Va.].

Sabbath, 7. I changed my subject after getting into the church; and I spoke long and plainly. We have news from the English Conference. It has given me an invitation to my native land, engaging to pay the expenses of the visit.

Thursday, April 8. Spring has at last returned—a treble spring—natural, spiritual, and political. What a winter we have gone through! what weather for five months! what roads!

Saturday, May 15. We toiled over the rocky road to Haverstraw [New York], sixteen miles; and I delivered my testimony in great feebleness of body. We lodged with Peter Noyelle. Our host built his house for a tavern, but it was turned into a church. At Philipstown we have an elegant new chapel; I preached in it on Monday, and felt liberty in the Word.

Tuesday, 18. Came to Richard Jackson's, twenty-five miles. I was required to preach at a minute's warning, as I found an assembly ready. It would seem as if the preachers think they are committing a sin if they do not appoint preaching for me every day, and often twice a day. Lord, support us in our labour, and we will not murmur.

Sunday, June 6. Knowing the uncertainty of the tenure of life, I have made my will, appointing Bishop M'Kendree, Daniel Hitt, and Henry Boehm, my executors. If I do not in the meantime spend it, I shall leave, when I

THE BEAUTIFUL CATSKILLS

BROADWAY, NEW YORK, N.Y., ca. 1819

VIEW OF HUDSON AND THE CATSKILL MOUNTAINS

die, an estate of two thousand dollars, I believe: I give it all to the Book Concern. . . . Let it all return, and continue to aid the cause of piety.

Tuesday, June 8. We have had pleasing rains, and nature begins to put on her charms. My mind enjoys a constant serenity, whether labouring or at rest, in ease or pain. "To me to live is Christ; to die is gain."

Wednesday, 30. It is surprising to see the improvement of the city of Hudson in twenty years. We have spent about ten dollars a month, as road expenses; but where are our clothing and our horses to come from; what have we left for charity? It must be gotten from two hundred dollars, allowed us by the conference. But may we not beg? For ourselves—no.

Thursday, July 22. The horse in the sulky has his shoulder swelled. Brother M'Kendree's beast dragged me over a rough path to Bowman's. My face and teeth are in great pain and disorder.

Friday, 23. Great suffering from pain in my face. Saturday, I preached and retired in a high fever to take medicine, and to blister my face. . . . I am alive, however; and some of the good folks of Philadelphia and Jersey have said they should never see Francis again. In the midst of all our suffering and disappointment, God is with us.

Wednesday, August 11. . . . Thy quiet dust is not called to the labour of riding five thousand miles in eight months—to meet ten conferences in a line of sessions from the District of Maine, to the banks of the Cayuga—to the States of Ohio, of Tennessee, of Mississippi—to Cape Fear, James River, Baltimore, Philadelphia, and to the completion of the round. . . . Lord, be with us, and help us to fulfil the task thou hast given us to perform!

1814 *Sunday, April 24. I return to my journal after an interval of twelve weeks. I have been ill indeed, but medicine, nursing, and kindness under God, have been so far effectual, that I have recovered strength enough to sit in my little covered wagon, into which they lift me. I have clambered over the rude mountains, passing through York and Chambersburg to Greensburg.*

Tuesday, July 19. My friends in Philadelphia gave me a light, little four-wheeled carriage; but God and the Baltimore Conference made me a richer present—they gave me John Wesley Bond as a travelling companion; has he his equal on the earth for excellencies of every kind as an aid? I groan one minute with pain, and shout glory the next!

Saturday, 23. Pittsburgh. We have made three hundred and fifty miles since we left Jersey. What roads! It was the mercy of Providence, or we should have been dashed to pieces. My body is, nevertheless, in better health; and my mind and soul happy and confident in God.

Sabbath, October 30. I passed a restless, feverish night; yet as I was expected to preach on the camp ground, I discoursed to a large, simple-hearted congregation, on Acts xxx, 32. I sat in the end of my little Jersey wagon, screened by the drawn curtain behind me.

Friday, December 9. I preached at Bethlehem to about three hundred souls. . . . By letter from John Earley we have great accounts of the work of God at camp meetings in Amelia and Prince Edward [Virginia].

THE CRUDE STATE OF WESTERN ROADS

"The news has reached us of the descent of the British in Maryland, and the burning of the public buildings at Washington."
Journals, September 9, 1814

"O SAY CAN YOU SEE . . ."—BOMBARDMENT ON BALTIMORE. THE BATTLE WHICH INSPIRED
FRANCIS SCOTT KEY TO WRITE "THE STAR-SPANGLED BANNER."

A SLAVE WHIPPING

A FRONTIER RESIDENCE

1815 _Monday, January 9. I bled in the arm to relieve the spitting of blood. This place [Charleston, S.C.] calls for great labour, and I am not fit for it: I must go hence._

Saturday, 14. Away with the false cant, that the better you use Negroes the worse they will use you! Make them good, then—teach them the fear of God, and learn to fear him yourselves, ye masters! I understand not the doctrine of cruelty. As soon as the poor Africans see me, they spring with life to the boat, and make a heavy flat skim along like a light canoe: poor starved souls—God will judge!

Saturday, 28. My trust is in a faithful God—He hath never deceived nor forsaken me. _I am scarcely an hour free from pain, and all that I do is in the strength of Jesus._

Monday, 30. Cold, indeed; my feet suffer. We made twenty-six miles to a house—no wood at the door, and none to cut wood.

Tuesday, 31. A heavy snow storm took us at Greenville [N.C.]. We put the remains of a poor, pious slave in the ground who had reached 100 years.

Sunday, February 26. Thanks to the God of peace! we are confirmed in the belief that a treaty has been made between the United States and Great Britain.

Friday, March 3. As we passed Monticello, a cloud rested upon it: the day was clear. We crossed the north

MONTICELLO—HOME OF THOMAS JEFFERSON

branch of James River, near Charlottesville. Sheltered for the night, under the roof of the widow Gillum. We have had bad roads, and I am feebleness itself.

Saturday, March 18. I preached at the Point [Baltimore]. Our conference began on Monday, and prudence restrained me to one session per day; perhaps I did not speak officially six times during the continuance of the conference. When it was understood that the ancient superintendent did not attend in the afternoon, the visits to him were renewed. Stationing about eighty-five preachers we found to be no small work.

ALBANY ABOUT 1823

HOUSE OF DUTCH GOVERNORS, ALBANY

Sunday, 26. At Eutaw Chapel, I spoke upon the apostolic order of things. Monday, conference rose. Tuesday, I retired to Perry Hall.

Friday, May 19, a cold rain dogged us into Albany. Saturday, I paid an hour's visit to my brethren in conference.

Sunday, 21. By vote of conference, I preached the funeral sermon for Doctor Coke—of blessed mind and soul—of the third branch of Oxonian Methodists—a gentleman, a scholar, and a bishop, to us—and as a minister of Christ, in zeal, in labours, and in services, the greatest man in the last century. Poor wheezing, groaning, coughing Francis visited the conference chamber on Tuesday and Thursday. Although confined to my room, I was not prevented from entering deeply into the consideration of the plan of the stations: the elders thought I came out well. Alas! what miseries and distresses are here. How shall we meet the charge of seventy married out of ninety-five preachers—children—sick wives—and the claims of conference? We are deficient in dollars and discipline.

THE LAST DAYS

On Thursday, December 7, 1815, Asbury penned the following words: "We met a storm and stopped at William Baker's, Granby." With this line, Asbury ended his journal of forty-five years.

His health wasted, Asbury knew death was imminent. Still he tried valiantly to keep his appointments. Asbury wanted to finish his ministry as it had begun—on the long road!

Between January and March, 1816, Asbury made a final journey across North and South Carolina and into Virginia. Though too feeble to write, he dictated several letters to his friends, and prepared an address which he hoped to deliver at the ensuing General Conference. Asbury never delivered this address. On Sunday, March 31, 1816, Asbury departed the land of his labor for his eternal home.

In 1821, Francis Hollingsworth, the editor of Asbury's posthumously published journal, wrote a description of the late bishop's final days. The following is an extract from Hollingsworth's "A Short Account of His Death."

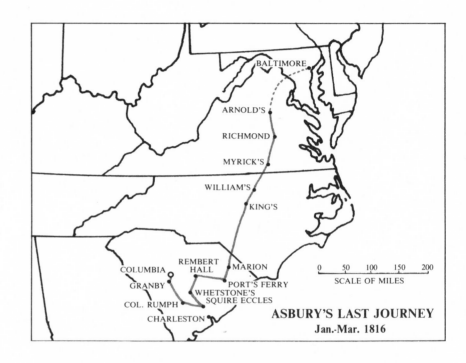

ASBURY'S LAST JOURNEY
Jan.-Mar. 1816

"A Short Account of His Death"

It seems that, notwithstanding his extreme debility, . . . he flattered himself with the prospect of meeting the ensuing General Conference, which was to assemble in Baltimore on the 2d of May, 1816. In this expectation he was, however, disappointed; the disease with which he was afflicted, terminating in the consumption, made such rapid progress as to baffle the power of medicine, and to prostrate the remaining strength of a constitution already trembling under the repeated strokes of disease, and worn down by fatigue and labour. He appeared, indeed, more like a walking skeleton than like a living man.

His great mind, however, seemed to rise superior to his bodily weakness, and to bid defiance to the hasty approaches of dissolution. Hence, impelled on by that unquenchable thirst to do good, . . . he continued with his faithful travelling companion, John W. Bond, in a close carriage, to journey from place to place, as his exhausting strength would permit, frequently preaching, until he came to Richmond, Virginia, where he preached his last sermon, March 24, 1816, in the old Methodist church.

After having delivered his testimony, he was carried from the pulpit to his carriage, and he rode to his lodgings.

On Tuesday, Thursday, and Friday, he journeyed, and finally came to the house of his old friend, Mr. George Arnold, in Spottsylvania. It was his intention to have reached Fredericksburg, about twenty miles farther, but the weather being unfavourable, and his strength continuing to fail, he was compelled to relinquish his design, and accordingly he remained under the hospitable roof of his friend, Mr. Arnold. . . .

About eleven o'clock on Sabbath morning, he inquired if it was not time for meeting; but recollecting himself, he requested the family to be called together. This being done agreeably to his request, brother Bond sang, prayed, and expounded the twenty-first chapter of the Apocalypse. During these religious exercises he appeared calm and much engaged in devotion. After this, such was his weakness, he was unable to swallow a little barley water which was offered to him, and his speech began to fail. Observing the distress of brother Bond, he raised his dying hand, at the same time looking joyfully at him. On being asked by brother Bond if he felt the Lord Jesus to be precious, exerting all his remaining strength, he in token of complete victory, raised both his hands. A few minutes after, as he sat on his chair, with his

This closed his public labours on the earth. The audience was much affected. Indeed, how could it be otherwise? To behold a venerable old man, under the dignified character of an ecclesiastical patriarch, whose silver locks indicated that time had already numbered his years, and whose pallid countenance and trembling limbs presaged that his earthly race was nearly finished: to see in the midst of these melancholy signals of decaying nature, a soul beaming with immortality, and a heart kindled with divine fire from the altar of God: —to see such a man, and to hear him address them in the name of the Lord of hosts, on the grand concerns of time and eternity! . . .

THE HOME OF GEORGE ARNOLD IN SPOTTSYLVANIA COUNTY, VIRGINIA, WHERE BISHOP ASBURY DIED

head reclined on the hand of brother Bond, without a struggle and with great composure, he breathed his last, on Sabbath, the 21st day of March, in the year of our Lord 1816, and in the seventy-first year of his age. . . .

His immortal spirit having taken its flight to the regions of the blessed, his body was committed to the earth, being deposited in the family burying ground of Mr. Arnold, in whose house he died. His remains were, by order of the General Conference, and at the request of the society of Baltimore, taken up and brought to that city, and deposited in a vault prepared for that purpose, under the recess of the pulpit of the Methodist church in Eutaw Street. A vast concourse of the citizens of Baltimore, with several clergymen of other denominations, followed the corpse as it was carried from the General Conference room in Light Street to the place prepared for its reception in Eutaw Street; being preceded by Bishop M'Kendree as the officiating minister, and brother Black, a representative from the British to the American Conference, and followed by the members of the General Conference as chief mourners. The corpse was placed in Eutaw church, and a funeral oration pronounced by the Rev. William M'Kendree, the only surviving bishop; after which the body of this great man of God was deposited in the vault, to remain until the resurrection of the just and unjust.* . . .

THE MONUMENTS TO JESSE LEE,
ROBERT STRAWBRIDGE, AND BISHOPS
ASBURY, GEORGE, EMORY, AND WAUGH.
MOUNT OLIVET CEMETERY, BALTIMORE, MD.

OLD EUTAW M.E. CHURCH, 1816

May that Church which so long enjoyed the services of this eminent minister of the sanctuary, and for whose prosperity he so diligently and conscientiously toiled and suffered, not only cherish a grateful remembrance of his Christian and ministerial virtues, but be long blessed with a succession of ministers who shall make his virtues their exemplar, and transmit to posterity unsullied those pure doctrines of Christ which Francis Asbury so faithfully and so successfully proclaimed.

*In June, 1854, Asbury's remains were transferred to the Mount Olivet Cemetery in Baltimore.

THE LEGACY

By the time of Asbury's death, the Methodist Episcopal Church included some 215,000 members and ranked first in size among Protestant denominations in America. This was an impressive accomplishment for a religious body less than half a century old.

Over the ensuing years the Methodist movement splintered into a variety of denominational organizations. Though different in many ways, every member of the Methodist family shares a common heritage, and this heritage is the legacy of Bishop Francis Asbury—the father of American Methodism.

Below are extracts from the address Asbury prepared, yet did not live to deliver. Its words remain a challenge for those who in the Wesleyan and Asburian tradition aspire to spread "scriptural holiness across the land."

A "SADDLE-BAGS MAN"

Introduction to Asbury's Address to the 1816 General Conference

Most dearly beloved in the Lord:

My loving confidential sons in the Gospel of the grace of God, in Christ Jesus, great grace rest upon you. The God of glory cover your assembly and direct all your acts and deliberations for the Apostolic order and establishment of the Church of God in holy succession to the end of time. Only recollect as far as your observation or information will go, what God hath done by us in Europe and America in about 70 years in Europe, and less than 50 years in America, and what wonderful things He may do for us and our successors in future years if we stand fast in the Gospel doctrine and pure Apostolic ordination, discipline and government into which we have been called and now stand.

Asbury's Requisites for Methodist Bishops

They must be formed in all things after the pattern shewed us in the mount, able Ministers of the New Testament, real Apostolic men filled with the Holy Ghost. But what does our order of things require of them? Not such as can be performed by superannuated or super-numerary preachers, but by men just past the meridian, that have already proved themselves not only servants but mere slaves, who with willing minds have taken with cheerfulness and resignation frontier stations, with hard fare, labouring and suffering night and day. . . . They ought to be men who can ride at least three thousand miles and meet ten or eleven Conferences in a year, . . . ready for all the duties of their calling, always pleasant, affable, and communicative—to know how to behave in all company, rich and poor, impious or pious, ministers and professors of our own and all denominations, but more abundantly to remember to the poor the gospel must always be preached, and always to condescend to men of low estate.

TEN EARLY AMERICAN METHODIST BISHOPS

JOSHUA SOULE

THOMAS COKE

PHILIP WILLIAM OTTERBEIN

ELIJAH HEDDING

FRANCIS ASBURY

RICHARD WHATCOAT

ROBERT ROBERTS

JACOB ALBRIGHT

ENOCH GEORGE

WILLIAM McKENDREE

DESCENDANTS of BISHOP ASBURY (A PARTIAL LISTING)

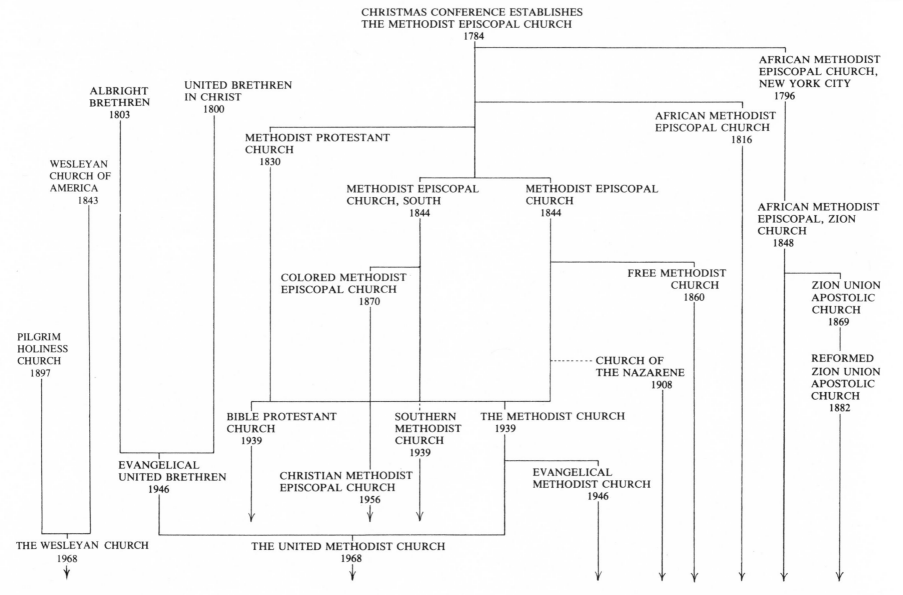

CHRISTMAS CONFERENCE ESTABLISHES
THE METHODIST EPISCOPAL CHURCH
1784

AFRICAN METHODIST
EPISCOPAL CHURCH,
NEW YORK CITY
1796

ALBRIGHT
BRETHREN
1803

UNITED BRETHREN
IN CHRIST
1800

AFRICAN METHODIST
EPISCOPAL CHURCH
1816

METHODIST PROTESTANT
CHURCH
1830

WESLEYAN
CHURCH OF
AMERICA
1843

METHODIST EPISCOPAL
CHURCH, SOUTH
1844

METHODIST EPISCOPAL
CHURCH
1844

AFRICAN METHODIST
EPISCOPAL, ZION
CHURCH
1848

COLORED METHODIST
EPISCOPAL CHURCH
1870

FREE METHODIST
CHURCH
1860

ZION UNION
APOSTOLIC
CHURCH
1869

PILGRIM
HOLINESS
CHURCH
1897

CHURCH OF
THE NAZARENE
1908

REFORMED
ZION UNION
APOSTOLIC
CHURCH
1882

BIBLE PROTESTANT
CHURCH
1939

SOUTHERN
METHODIST
CHURCH
1939

THE METHODIST CHURCH
1939

EVANGELICAL
UNITED BRETHREN
1946

CHRISTIAN METHODIST
EPISCOPAL CHURCH
1956

EVANGELICAL
METHODIST CHURCH
1946

THE WESLEYAN CHURCH
1968

THE UNITED METHODIST CHURCH
1968

INDEX OF PLACES

INDEX OF MOUNTAINS, RIVERS, LAKES, AND STREAMS

INDEX OF PEOPLE